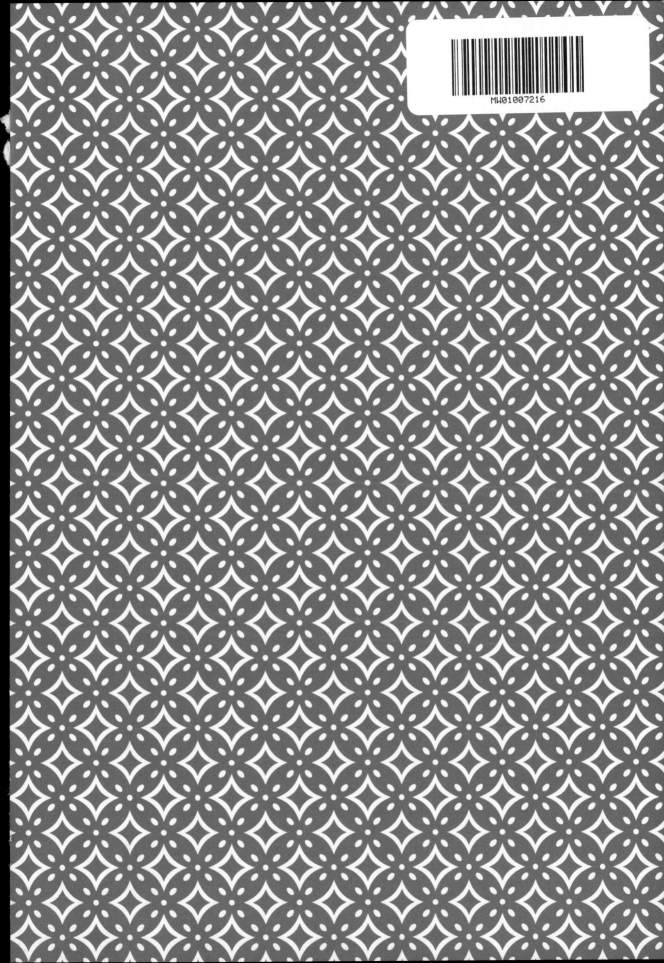

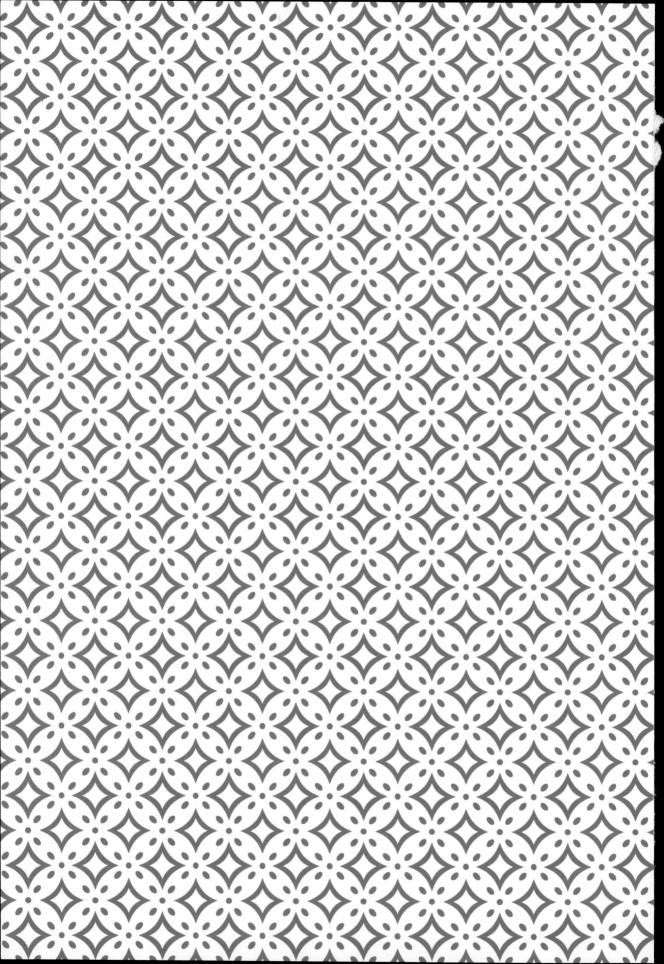

YOUR *Pasta* SUCKS

YOUR *Pasta* SUCKS

A "Cookbook"

MATTEO LANE

WITH **JJ GOODE**

PHOTOGRAPHY BY **ANTONIS ACHILLEOS**

CHRONICLE BOOKS

SAN FRANCISCO

Library of Congress Cataloging-in-Publication
Data available.

ISBN 978-1-7972-2956-0
ISBN (Signed Edition) 978-1-7972-3713-8

Manufactured in China.

MIX
Paper | Supporting
responsible forestry
FSC™ C008047

Food styling by Victoria Granof.
Prop styling by Emanuela Rota and
Christopher White.
Design by Michael Morris.
Typesetting by Wynne Au-Yeung.

10 9 8 7 6 5 4 3 2 1

Chronicle books and gifts are available
at special quantity discounts to corpora-
tions, professional associations, literacy
programs, and other organizations. For
details and discount information, please
contact our premiums department at
corporatesales@chroniclebooks.com
or at 1-800-759-0190.

Chronicle Books LLC
680 Second Street
San Francisco, California 94107
www.chroniclebooks.com

To you, Mom.

Contents

CHAPTER 1

Family

Introduction

I never meant to write a cookbook. Honestly, I probably should've written a book about love or Mariah Carey or *Fortnite*. I will say, though, that my romance with pasta has been my longest and best relationship. Pasta is exciting and comforting. Pasta is always there, right in your pantry. Pasta never ghosts you or lies about its size. Except for paccheri. Sometimes they're massive.

Also, pasta might just be the only thing I take seriously. Like most of my family, I will joke and laugh my way through just about anything, trauma included. We will all cackle when we tell stories of my Mexican grandfather, who had a secret family, including kids he gave the exact same names as his other kids, so he wouldn't accidentally give the game away. We all call him "The Hand," because my nonna cut him out of every photo so the only trace of him in albums is his hand. Believe it or not, I was even able to laugh about Britney's "comeback" at the 2007 VMAs, the one that started with a close-up of her poorly glued hair extensions. It took me a solid decade, but I got there.

But make me carbonara with cream or onions or peas and I'm as serious as the president in the Situation Room. Carbonara is the reason this cookbook exists. Carbonara, my mom, and my aunt Cindy. I didn't eat carbonara growing up. In Chicago in the nineties, there was mostly the red sauce bubbling in my aunt Cindy's cauldron and the Cherie Lane invention that I call Pasta della Mamma (page 34)— a melding of harried working mom and culinary genius.

We ate pasta at least three times a week. Sometimes it was dinner. Other nights it was *with* dinner, served alongside chicken cutlets or braciole. I think the only reason we didn't have pasta *every day* was because my dad is Irish and pasta, it should be noted, is neither steak nor potato. Every night, my brother, sister, and I—two-thirds of us gay, by the way—would follow my mother into the kitchen like ducklings and help her cook. This is how I got comfortable in the kitchen, by rolling meatballs and frying struffoli.

My affection for pasta only deepened when I left Chicago, first for trips to southern Italy, where I had my first dalliance with pesto trapanese, and then to Rome, where I fell head over high heels for real carbonara. The friends I made there, my Roman family, schooled me on the rules. Guanciale, not pancetta. Pecorino, not parm. Pasta cooked not "American" al dente (a.k.a. baby food) but Italian al dente (just a bit softer than grissini). And there is to be no cream or butter. The creaminess that makes real carbonara so good comes from the enchanted union of pork fat, egg, and starchy pasta water.

I learned to love how bitchy (or, fine, "particular") Italians are about their food. And how authenticity isn't about how they do it in Italy versus America. Instead, it's like this: Unless your grandma made the dish, then it's wrong, wrong, wrong. You used the incorrect pasta shape or added chile or didn't add chile—whatever you did, you've ruined it. I remember reading, for instance, that neighboring cities Bologna and Modena fight over who invented the tortellini. Basically, both camps agree the shape was modeled after some Renaissance-era hottie's belly button (supposedly an innkeeper was taken by it when he looked through a keyhole, like a peeping-Tommaso). So basically, horniness is confirmed as the inspiration, but the two camps diverge on where the horniness happened, and either way, in Modena you fold tortellini around your index finger while in Bologna, it's the pinkie. And everyone yells about it. Andy Cohen, greenlight *The Real Housewives Emilia-Romagna*, stat.

I've been known to be quite particular myself, so after years of eating and cooking and nurturing my own strong opinions about carbonara, I decided to make an Instagram video about the dish that had lost its way. I'm a big Food Network fan, or at least I was before every show became a battle to the death. Cupcakes Wars, Chocolate Wars, Chicken Wars. Can you imagine being a vet coming back from Iraq after three tours and being all, "War sucks" then some middle-aged woman from Minnesota's like, "I know! Sugar War 2018, I lost a foot." (Yes, that's a diabetes joke.)

But I didn't want to be all *The Great British Bake Off*, either, which I love because everyone is so nice. I'm not that nice. Anyway, I post my video and the next morning, I wake up and the first comment is so long it looks like a CVS receipt. The poster liked the video, but . . . "My heart ached," they wrote, "when I saw you throwing away the egg whites. You must consider keeping the egg whites in a bowl and giving it to someone who needs it." Imagine. Me walking down six flights of stairs from my apartment carrying a bowl filled with three egg whites. And if you don't know those are egg whites in that bowl, then I'm just transporting something really suspicious looking. Finally, I get downstairs and approach the first person I see with my bowl, like, "Here you go, drink up."

Aside from the occasional concerned citizen, not to mention a few sweethearts chiming in to remind me that I'm going to hell, people liked the video. So, I made more. And sometimes I invited people to join in—from friends who have taught me to cook to fellow comedians, who are monsters who can barely boil water. Millions of views later, I'm writing a cookbook. Throughout the process, I wondered, *Should I even be writing a cookbook?* I'm an amateur opera singer. I'm a School of the Art Institute of Chicago grad who's painted a mural for the Obamas (no big deal). I've been doing stand-up, mostly in obscurity until recently, for the past fifteen years. But a cookbook author? That's not me, I decided, when it was already too late to stop.

Another obstacle is that I'm Italian, which means that until I was forced to write recipes, I had never measured anything in my life. Italians don't use 1.37 cups of pecorino. We just add pecorino by the handful until the dish looks right. But for you, I dusted off my measuring cups and spoons in an effort to show you that cooking isn't scary, that you can absolutely cook delicious pasta at home. Pasta, like hang gliding, can be safe and fun, as long as you follow a few rules. We're not throwing spaghetti at the ceiling or dumping sauce on naked pasta like an old Ragú commercial, people.

I get it, if you didn't grow up rolling meatballs, cooking can be a little scary, especially the first few times—like me going to the gym for the first time, standing next to guys who looked like centaurs while I was wearing my Janet Jackson T-shirt. My main goal is to help up your pasta game without getting canceled by a guy from Cefalù because

I suggest the wrong tube-shaped pasta. My actual nightmare is to be stitched by some Italian chef TikTokker who reacts to me using Pecorino Romano in a Sicilian pasta as if I were trying to diffuse a bomb and just cut the wrong wire.

The book begins with some basics, then moves on to recipes for pastas and a few other dishes that I've learned to cook over the years from my family and friends. My repertoire is limited by my knowledge and preference. I'm not an expert in baked ziti, for example, because my aunt Cindy makes the best and only baked mostaccioli I need. I'm not into puttanesca—too much going on. I don't eat sea creatures since my last bite of octopus sent me to the hospital. So don't expect something comprehensive. Just some great food and stories to wash it down.

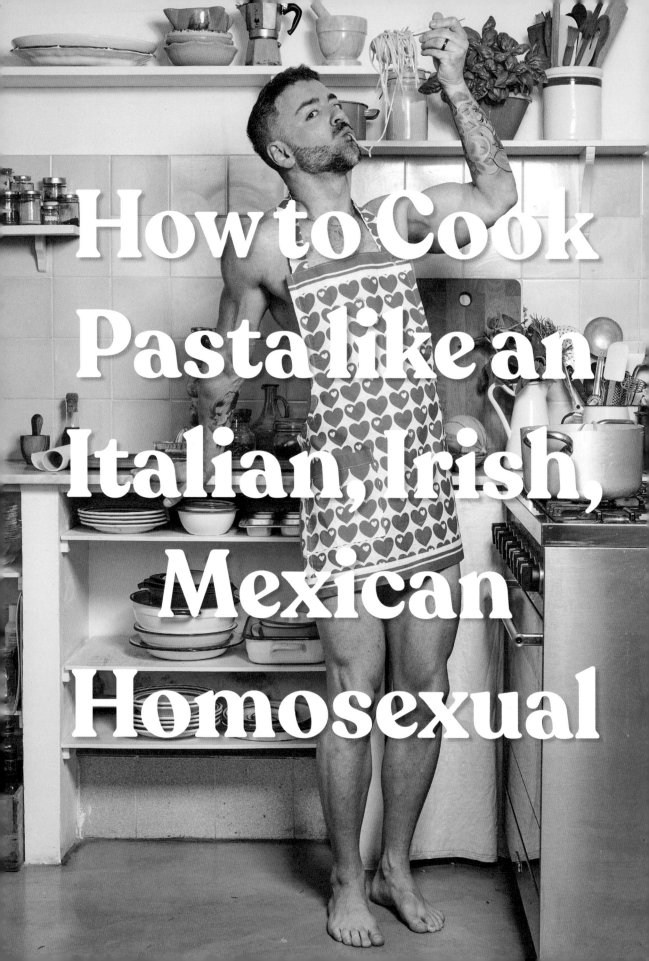

How to Cook Pasta like an Italian, Irish, Mexican Homosexual

If you are anything like my friends, your pasta game is a disaster. **You need a little guidance, and I'm here to give it. Before you start following recipes, you need a rundown of some common ingredients and a primer on pasta making, so you don't screw up.**

Pasta Pantry

BASIL: I'm not here to tell you to seek out Genovese basil or grow your own. Actually, I have nothing to say about basil, other than, obviously, buy fresh basil and do not store it in the fridge. I don't know why but the fridge turns the leaves black and gross. To avoid that happening, store it stems first in a glass with water, covered loosely with a plastic bag, on your counter.

CHEESE: There is a vast universe of Italian cheese, but you can make approximately a million pasta dishes with just these four: Parmigiano-Reggiano, Pecorino Romano, ricotta, and mozzarella.

Parmigiano-Reggiano, a.k.a. Parmesan, is the real thing, the genuine article, the product that earns the title "King of Cheese." In fact, we're not even going to shorten it to "Parmesan" in this book, since you can buy domestic "Parmesan" that tastes like it's made in Trenton, New Jersey, not to mention the sawdust in those green cans at the grocery store. The name Parmigiano-Reggiano is literally regulated by the Italian government. (See? Italian politicians do more than just the bribe-taking and orgy-having that you read about in the news.) This cheese can save any dish. Pasta's overcooked? Add Parmigiano-Reggiano. Undersalted? Add Parmigiano-Reggiano. Over salted? Add Parmigiano-Reggiano. I swear, it's salty or sweet when it needs to be. Just like my aunt Cindy.

Pecorino Romano, the cheese of choice in Roman pasta cookery, was a common sight in my family's fridge growing up. She's aged sheep's cheese and she tastes like it—she's especially salty, tangy, and even kind of spicy. As with Parmigiano-Reggiano, accept no imitations.

Mozzarella, we all know and love. You can totally buy the low-moisture kind (sold in firm blocks rather than squishy balls) for the recipes in this book, but I prefer the flavor of those freshly made spheres. When necessary, give the mozzarella a good squeeze to drain the excess moisture that might make, say, lasagna or baked mostaccioli watery.

Ricotta is a cheese we grew up making ourselves (see Kate's Ricotta, page 57), but there's zero shame in buying it. Just make sure you seek out one from a proper Italian market or at least from a grocery store with a solid cheese section. You want ricotta that's milky-sweet and creamy with tender curds, not the stuff that tastes like mislabeled cottage cheese you find at most supermarkets.

And just please don't buy pre-grated cheese. It's bad. And not just that. It's often more expensive by the pound *and* it's bad. It has this plasticky quality, like someone took a box grater to a Barbie.

GUANCIALE AND PANCETTA: Two forms of pig salt, basically. Guanciale is pork jowl that's cured with salt and spices. Pancetta is pork belly that's cured with salt and spices. They're both nice and fatty, with guanciale being only about 3% *not* fat.

And no, substituting bacon is unacceptable. Bacon is smoked. Bacon is cured with different seasonings. So just stop. Also, while we're on the subject, stop buying bad supermarket pancetta. You want to buy pancetta from the kind of market where salami hangs from the ceiling or at least a store that has at minimum one full wheel of Parmigiano-Reggiano on hand. And honestly, you'll only find guanciale in markets that sell things like cardoon honey and Sicilian jarred cherry tomatoes that cost as much as a New York City martini.

Don't buy it pre-sliced or chopped. Be sure to carve off the tough skin before using.

OLIVE OIL: You're not Oprah. You can't afford oil that's crafted by husband-and-wife olive farmers or tastes like freshly cut Tuscan grass. Your apartment should not look like the Museum of Olive Oil. Just get a nice big bottle from the supermarket that's not so cheap it's suspicious. Plus, the good stuff isn't for cooking anyway. It's for "finishing," or so Food Network tells me. Well, I'm only thirty-seven, so I finish just fine for now, thank you.

PASTA WATER: Yes, this is an ingredient and as vital to good pasta as Parmigiano-Reggiano and olive oil. But you can't buy it, so you've got to make it. If I could, I'd store it and put it next to the salt and pepper, it's that essential. So, after you cook pasta, make sure you reserve some of the acqua di cottura, which is what Italians call the salty, murky water.

When you cook pasta, especially high-quality pasta, in salty boiling water, it sheds some of its starch and transforms into this mystical potion that makes almost any pasta dish better. When you add the starchy water to whatever you're saucing your pasta with—whether that's red sauce, ragù, or guanciale fat—the result is a sauce that clings to and coats your pasta in a creamy, silky way. Basically, the starch helps water and fat join forces, or "emulsify," which is a word food people seem to use when they're trying to sound like they know things, so I'm doing it, too, now that I'm officially a cookbook author.

It's especially important in certain dishes like pasta aglio e olio or pasta alla gricia—that is,

dishes in which the sauce is as simple as just oil or rendered fat—so you'll see that some recipes call for less boiling water for the pasta than others. That way, the water ends up starchier.

And when you properly salt your pasta water, the salt infuses into the pasta itself, so your sauce isn't the only source of seasoning. How salty should it be, you ask? More than you think but less than you're often told. I've seen friends add anything from zero salt to four grains of salt, which isn't even close. You want a good handful in your pasta pot full of water. But do you want it salty as the sea, as so many recipes advise? Absolutely not. Bleh, can you imagine? Are you all swimming in different seas than me, what's happening here? If you're the measuring type, go for 2 tablespoons of salt for *every* quart of water. Or just add a handful of salt and taste the water—you want it to taste as salty as a soup you get at a diner that makes you think, *Hmm, this needs a little salt.*

SALT: Speaking of salt, the salt you currently use is probably the salt you should keep using. Don't go mixing things up just for fun, because salts of different brands and types and shapes have a wildly different effect on your food. Maybe you always cook with Diamond Crystal kosher salt, then one day you're at a friend's place making dinner and all they have is Morton. You add the same big pinch to your ragù that you normally do, and it's ruined.

This also means that if you use a different salt than I do, the recipes will turn out differently. So let me say that when my friend JJ, whom I am 100 percent grateful for and definitely do not resent, insisted that I measure every last pinch of salt I used for the recipes in this book, I used Diamond Crystal. So there.

TOMATO PASSATA: Whenever I use this jarred product around my friend Nick, who is the queen of Prego, he says, "See, you're also using jarred sauce." No, Nick, you monster, tomato passata is strained tomato purée and contains just tomatoes, a little salt, and sometimes basil. Prego's third ingredient is sugar. Tomato passata has a lovely pure tomato flavor, and since it's strained, there's no trace of bitterness from the seeds. I always buy jars of the Mutti brand, but you do you.

Pasta

First things first: Fresh pasta is not better than dried pasta—it's *different*. There are dishes that are best made with fresh pasta and there are dishes that are best made with dried, because they're different. Fresh pasta, often made with egg, has a richer flavor and more delicate texture. Dried pasta is more neutral in flavor but can achieve that glorious al dente bite.

Is my friend Elena serving ragù with dried spaghetti? No. Instead, she's going to be tenderly tossing her ragù with fresh tagliatelle or pappardelle. Are you ever going to see fresh pasta alla carbonara, gricia, or amatriciana? Not unless you're in hell, in which case you have bigger problems than pasta. Meanwhile, cacio e pepe is made with both dried and fresh pasta, but don't ask me why. I can only share the rules. I don't make them.

All that is to say, follow the rules and don't get cute unless you really know what you're doing, which you probably don't since here you are preparing to follow a stand-up comedian's recipes.

Buying Pasta

You should try to make fresh pasta, because it's fun and not particularly difficult if you have an inexpensive pasta machine. You can also buy it, though the quality will vary widely depending on where you get it. Buy it somewhere that makes it in-house or where the people selling it seem like they'd have strong opinions about the ingredients they'd put in a ragù. You should not, on the other hand, make dried pasta. That's way harder. So definitely buy it. De Cecco is just fine, but get yourself to a nice market (or to an online one like gustiamo.com) and buy pasta that has been cut with a bronze die, dried slowly, and priced high enough to make you feel slightly guilty for splurging. Good dried pasta doesn't fall apart in the pot. It gives you starchier pasta water. It makes dinner better for science-y reasons. And come on, some people drop forty dollars a pound on steak but won't spend ten dollars on a box of well-made pasta? Madness.

Pasta Shapes

There are approximately one million pasta shapes. There is pastina, which is basically just a pasta speck, and there is candele, which is long and girthy (I said what I said). There are pasta tubes of varying lengths and widths. There are shapes that are long and thin, long and flat, long and squared off at the edges, long and rounded at the edges, long and hollow, long and curly, long and curly and hollow. There are pasta of the same shape that have different names because one has ridges, and another doesn't. And they all have different monikers and highly specific purposes. Often, there's a logic to it, but sometimes the reason is because Nonna says so.

Since we're not eighty-eight-year-olds living in Modena, we get to abide by our own logic and have our own preferences. For example, I am all about spaghetti. If there's a choice, I'm choosing it, just like when I'm playing *Super Mario Bros. 2* for NES, I'm choosing Mario.

Both are straightforward. They're down to earth. They get the job done. They're not flashy. We're not choosing rotini, just like we're not selecting Princess Peach. But let's be honest. I always played as Princess Peach.

Rigatoni is also great. Which isn't news. I mean, everyone loves it. On Sundays my three thousand cousins and I would take a vote on which pasta we wanted to eat for dinner, and whatever I chose (probably spaghetti) always lost to rigatoni. I get it. It's a lovely little tube and holds sauce well.

For fresh pasta, I'm looking at long, flat pastas like fettuccine, tagliatelle, and pappardelle. The wider the pasta, the more fun we're having. They're all delightful to twist onto your fork. It's like eating streamers.

Some pasta shapes, however, need to mind their own business. I'm talking to you, linguine. Who do you think you are? You're not Squirtle or Blastoise—you're Wartortle. You're halfway between spaghetti and fettuccine. You're long and thin but also a little flat. Pick a lane. I don't associate with farfalle, either. It's for pasta salads and children who like to pretend they're eating a bowl of their dad's bowties. And it's a no for angel hair, which I call devil hair. It's too thin. You cook it for 0.05 seconds too long, and it goes from the golden locks of a heavenly messenger to angel pubes you'd find in your bathtub drain. It's so hard to control, and honestly every time I cook it and mess up, it feels personal. It's almost as if you can hear each hair laughing at me.

Here's How to Cook Pasta

Yes, you'll be following the recipes themselves, and yes, they'll sometimes deviate slightly from the steps you see here. But this is the big-picture process for making pasta, which you can apply to improve your own cooking adventures.

First, bring a pot of water to a boil. While it's coming to a boil, you can make your sauce, grate cheese, scroll, whatever. You might start thinking about how you can time things so that the saucy stuff is ready around the same time as the pasta. But remember, once you add the pasta to the water, the clock's ticking.

Great, the water is boiling. Now we're seasoning it—properly, people—with a nice handful of salt.

Now add the pasta. If you're working with short shapes (rigatoni, fusilli, orecchiette), stir for a few seconds. If you're cooking long, thin pasta that doesn't quite fit in the pot, let it soften slightly, then gently ease them into the water so they're submerged. Either way, stir occasionally while they cook. This way, the pasta won't stick to each other.

Success rides on serving the pasta when it still has that lovely bite. Sometimes, you'll cook the pasta to al dente in the boiling water, then toss it with your sauce (e.g. carbonara, pesto). Sometimes, you're going to undercook the pasta by two minutes or so, then finish the cooking in the sauce (e.g. amatriciana, pomodoro), so the pasta absorbs the flavors. If you're as distractable as I am, you'll set a timer based on the pasta package instructions, just so you don't forget about it altogether. Then you'll try a piece. Because there's no "trick" to tell when it's ready. You're not going to toss it against the ceiling or slice it and assess the cross section. Just taste it, you maniacs.

When the timer goes off, you have two options for getting the pasta out of the water. 1) Drain the pasta in a colander BUT ONLY AFTER you scoop out and reserve a cup or so of the salty, starchy, magical, mystical pasta water or 2) use tongs (ideal for long, thin shapes) or a spider strainer (best for shorter shapes) to move the pasta from the pot to the pan with the sauce, which saves you a colander to wash and leaves you with enough acqua di cottura to sell on Etsy.

Once the pasta is in the pan with the sauce, add some of that pasta water (½ cup [120 ml] is usually a good start), then toss it gently but thoroughly to coat it well. Now you're going to give it a couple of minutes, stirring and tossing frequently, to finish cooking the pasta to that al dente texture and to allow the starchy water to meld with the sauciness so it enrobes the pasta rather than slipping off. As it cooks, gradually add more pasta water to keep the sauce nice and loose.

Now, it's time to taste, adjust the salt, and get the pasta into bowls or plates.

Al Dente

Nothing showcases the difference between Italian pasta and American pasta quite like the concept of al dente. The term, which translates as "to the tooth" and applies to dried pasta, is commonplace—open any cookbook, look on the back of any box of dried pasta—but let me tell you, you barely need teeth to eat the baby food that passes for spaghetti alla carbonara in most places in the United States, New York City included. You're not meant to gum pasta. You're also not going for the "slight bite" that sometimes serves as the English equivalent of "al dente." In Italy, and Rome in particular, I've had pasta with such a bite you wonder whether someone boiled it or fried it. You really do want that firmness in the center. Loving it requires initiation for Americans. Once you try, I doubt you'll ever go back.

How to Ruin Pasta

Just as I've shared what to do to make perfect pasta, I need to make sure you understand some of the things you should not do. Because I've seen what some of you do, and, well, we need to fix all that.

PLEASE: We're not doing one-pot pastas. This is a thing you see now, where you cook dried pasta, water, and who knows what else in a single pot until it's supposedly fit for dinner. I do not approve. Not all rules are meant to be broken. We're not sacrificing centuries of tradition just so we only have to wash one pot instead of two.

JUST STOP: Never, ever put oil in your pasta water. The theory is that the oil prevents the pasta from sticking together. Well, the pasta won't stick if you just occasionally stir while it's cooking, so do that instead. If the olive oil in the water does anything, it makes the cooked pasta so slick your sauce slips right off.

NO: Whatever you do, do not break the pasta so they fit in the pot—have you ever seen that TikTok where the woman breaks spaghetti in front of her Italian fiancé and he reacts like he'd seen her strangle a priest? That's me, but with more high-pitched screaming.

DON'T: Do not drown your pasta in sauce. In Italy, pasta dishes are about THE PASTA. Shocker, I know. The sauce is a condiment to the main event. It's a glaze that coats each strand. Think about pasta the way you think about steak. We're not cooking and seasoning something to perfection only to submerge it in soup. That said, Italian American households do engage in much saucier situations, but that's because we're monsters.

CUT IT OUT: When you're finally sitting down to a delicious plate of pasta, thoughtfully cooked and judiciously sauced, please do not reach for a knife. You do not need to cut your pasta. Please recall that you have teeth. I saw a couple once sit down at a really nice restaurant and after their pasta pomodoro arrived, they oohed and aahed and proceeded to slice the spaghetti. I swear I almost flipped the table.

CHAPTER 1

Family

THREE GREAT GRANDMAS AND TWENTY-SIX COUSINS

I learned to **cook, squabble,** and **crack jokes** in a three-bedroom Ranch-style house in Arlington Heights, a suburb of Chicago.

When I was older, I asked my mom, "Ma, did we not have money?"

And she goes, "I wouldn't say we didn't have money . . . let's just say we were living paycheck to paycheck." Got it. While we were far from wealthy, we were rich in relatives. I mean, seriously, there were fifty of us all living within a ten-block radius. My mom was one of seven (well, technically, one of fifteen if you count the secret family, but we'll get to that later) and they all reproduced like rabbits, so I grew up besieged by aunts, uncles, cousins, and grandparents. This is probably why I don't want kids. The comedian Andrew Schultz asked me once, "Wait, you're Italian *and* Irish *and* Mexican and you don't want kids?" Correct. *Someone* had to stop us.

We were all so close that the distinctions blurred. My aunt Cindy's daughter, Megan, for example, is technically my cousin, but we spent so much time together that she may as well be my sister and she's definitely one of my best friends. Aunt Cindy lived next door to us—just two Italian Mexican women with Irish cops for husbands who drive Buicks and had a bunch of kids who are the same ages. Basically, the identical family one door down.

I'm very close to my grandparents, too. They will never die. I just told them this the other day. My nonna is eighty-eight. She can't walk well, but when she's seated, my god she looks sixty. And believe me, it's not diet keeping them going, because they both eat terribly. It's that my nonna keeps the air-conditioning on all year round, even in January. It's like low-tech cryonics, though I guess they're more refrigerated than frozen.

On Sundays we would gather at Cindy's in the late afternoon, family members trickling in until there were anywhere from six to six hundred of us. My mom, Cherie, and Aunt Cindy would be at the stove stirring a cauldron of meat sauce, like Glinda and Elphaba, that had been bubbling since eight in the morning, the rest of us flitting around them grating cheese, slicing bread, making salad, or rolling meatballs. As a snack before dinner, us kids would raid the fridge for fresh mozzarella to tear up into pieces and dunk in the meat sauce.

At six in the evening, we ate and five minutes later my uncle Mike was cleaning up plates. My people would absolutely dominate at the Olympics of sprint eating. You'd think we'd be savoring every bite because we're so goddamn particular about what kind of cheese to tuck inside our braciole, but that's all eclipsed by our big-ass families all vying for a chunk of food. When there are twenty people at dinner, being full feels like winning. It's a survival instinct. We're like a pride of lions frantically gnawing on a downed gazelle.

OK, that's not quite true. Our eating was slowed by the fact that we screamed, nonstop, for four hours. It's not just that everyone's talking over one another. It's that you *have* to talk over one another. It's required. We all competed to tell the same stories, the family lore, repeated week after week, year after year. Joke for joke, nearly word for word, tweaked just slightly each time for effect—it was great practice for stand-up, actually. And at each telling, we'd all cackle like it was the first time we ever heard them.

In our loud family, Megan and I were the loudest. She did the best impression of her dad, my uncle Mike, brushing his teeth. It's so good. The man brushed his teeth so aggressively, like a mariner buffing the rust of a boat's hull, foam pouring down his arm. It's just a mess, partly because he refused to use the Dixie cups Aunt Cindy bought specifically to prevent said mess. So Megan's impersonating this, jamming an imaginary toothbrush in her mouth like she's deepthroating an Oral-B ProHealth and shouting in her dad's South Side Irish cop's drawl, "My father was in World War II and he didn't need any Dixie cups!" then switching to an impression of her mom, Cindy, yelling, "The war is over, Mike!" I needed Megan to do this while my uncle Mike was looking, and if he wasn't looking, I'd need her to do it again, and if he was finally looking and she was talking to someone else, I had to fix that through sheer volume.

In third grade, my class had to make a family tree. On the bottom, the teacher asked us to write what it means to be whatever we were. We were Italian, so I called my nonna and asked her, "Nonna, what does it mean to be Italian?" so I could write in her response, which I assumed would be something family or culture or food. The next day, I brought in my finished family tree, completed with my nonna's answer, and showed it to my teacher. On the bottom, it said, "I'm Italian because when everything's going well, something bad is going to happen."

I feel the exact same way today. Generational trauma, I suppose. Though give Nonna her due; her life has been much harder than mine, even if you count the day in 1996 when my neighbor Betty told my mom that she saw me in the backyard singing to birds "like a girl." ("He's even gayer than the other one," said Betty, the other one being my brother, who, yes, is also gay.) I mean, sure, while my sister Kate was out hunting with our dad (she can still skin a deer and butcher a pig) I was at home baking cookies with my mom and singing "I'm Wishing" from *Snow White* to some European starlings, so Betty was right, but Betty was also a bitch.

My grandma is Italian, raised on the South Side of Chicago. Her mom's family is from Naples, and well, we barely know a thing about them. When she was eighteen, she married a man named Joaquin Maldanado of Mexican heritage. They had seven kids, my mom included. My grandma told everyone her big, burly husband was a "bricklayer," but I get the sense he was doing less laying and more tying of bricks to people's feet. He was famous for leaving for a pack of cigarettes then not showing up again for six months.

Where was my grandpa, you're wondering? He was with his other family. Not only did he have another family, but he gave the kids on both sides of the family *the same names*. You know, so he wouldn't slip up. I was on a Mexican TV show once—it was hosted by a clown, literally, obviously. Of course, I told them the story of my grandpa and his secret family and the same kid names. Instead of reacting with appropriate horror, the host-clown immediately goes, "Your grandfather is very smart."

Well, my grandma finally ditched him. He was booted from the family and then erased. The moment my grandma got remarried to my current grandpa, a kind, blind Sicilian named Nick Pomaro, the moment her last name went from Maldonado to Pomaro, my first grandpa was *gone*. When Cindy and Cherie showed up to their new school that year, someone saw her and asked, "Hey, aren't you Cindy Maldonado?" And Cindy goes, "Nope," and walks away.

That means my mom and Cindy have three grandmas. And when you have three grandmas, it's tough to keep track of who you're talking about. So they got nicknames: Their mom's mom, we call This Gram and also Gram Gram. Their mom's husband's mom, we call That Gram. Their mom's first husband's mom, well, we never actually called her since that side of the family's excommunication, but when we refer to her, it's Nother Gram. If you're confused, good, because so am I.

The whole Mexican grandpa affair is just one of many family tragedies that we all mine for comedy when we get together. It's how we have always coped, recounting the worst details of our lives and laughing so hard we can't breathe. That's what we did. We talked and cooked and ate, and while we cooked and ate, we talked about what we had cooked and what we were eating or what we would cook and eat the next day or what we had cooked and eaten the day before.

We were almost always together, but even when it was just me and my siblings, food was entertainment. Cherie was our Barefoot Contessa.

My mom would cook meatballs and pizza and pasta—three times a week, at the very least—and wise woman she was, she'd have us watch. A great way for a busy mom without much money to keep the kids busy and get shit done. My sister, Kate, and I, in particular, both loved pulling up stools and watching red sauce simmer, meatballs get rolled, and pizza dough rise.

Because of Mom, we both love to cook and feel comfortable in the kitchen. It's why Kate is such a fantastic cook today, and it's why when I fell in love with Rome and its pastas, I learned to cook them well enough to impress my Roman friends. But as much as I adore cacio e pepe and amatriciana, there's still nothing like the red sauce Italian food of my family in Chicago.

Pasta della Mamma

Also known as pasta alla Cherie Lane.

My mom made this once a week when I was a kid. It was and still is my favorite pasta in the world. It exists nowhere besides my mom's and my sister's houses—at least, not until I made it on my YouTube channel, then you guys sent me pictures of you making it that I sent to my mom.

I don't know what possessed my mom to make this, but I bet it had something to do with having a full-time job, three hungry kids, and not much in the fridge, so she started digging into her pantry, like, *What can I feed these little monsters?* I guess you could call it pasta alla pantry. She mixed egg yolk, salted butter, 2 percent milk, Parmigiano-Reggiano, garlic powder, and pepper to a, frankly, rather unappealing paste. But when she added that paste to hot pasta, it melted to become a creamy, cheesy sauce that tastes like some Frankenstein version of carbonara, cacio e pepe, and alfredo.

Italians, I know. Cherie knows. So don't judge, Judy. Just try it.

4 tbsp [60 g] salted butter,
  at room temperature

1 large egg yolk, at room temperature

1 cup [100 g] finely grated (on a
  box grater) Parmigiano-Reggiano,
  at room temperature

¼ cup [60 ml] 2 percent milk,
  at room temperature

⅛ tsp freshly ground black pepper

⅛ tsp garlic powder

A handful of kosher salt, plus more
  as needed

8 oz [230 g] dried spaghetti
  (or whatever dried pasta you've got)

Bring a large pot of water to a boil.

In a medium bowl, add the butter and egg yolk and stir until smooth. If they're not combining that's because you didn't listen when I wrote room temperature, so don't come for me. Add the Parmigiano-Reggiano and stir again, until you've created a cheesy paste. Add the milk and stir, which will loosen the paste up a bit, and then season with the pepper and garlic powder. This is going to melt when it hits the hot pasta, just as I melted when I first saw my personal trainer.

Once the water is boiling, add the salt and then the spaghetti. Let the spaghetti soften slightly, then stir so the pasta doesn't stick together. Cook, stirring occasionally, until the pasta is al dente, about as long as the package instructions tell you, but the only way to tell for sure is to taste it yourself.

With a colander, drain the pasta, transfer the pasta back to the empty pot, and add the cheesy business (the butter mixture), stirring to coat the spaghetti in the sauce. The residual heat from the pasta will cook the egg yolk, so just relax. Season with salt.

Serve immediately and send any complaints to Cherie at gaywomb@aol.com.

Family Meat Sauce

MAKES ABOUT 3½ QUARTS [3.3 L]

I think Italian women and witches shop at the same stores.

Because every Sunday, when it was time to make sauce, my aunt Cindy would haul out a cauldron. This pot was HUGE. If there was a tornado, you could flip it over and hide an entire Italian family. When the rest of the coven, including my mom, made sauce, it was a by-the-gallons endeavor and would last all week.

For Cindy, making sauce is like breathing—you just do it. So asking for a "recipe" is like asking for instructions on how to inhale. Luckily, my gorgeous friend Elena, who lives in Rome and grew up in Milan, shared her recipe for a meaty ragù, which deviates just enough from traditional Bolognese to serve as an excellent stand-in for Cindy's sauce. If you love it, thank her. If not, blame me for ruining it.

Elena tenderly tosses hers with freshly made tagliatelle, which is, depending on the Italian you ask, the exact same thing as fettuccine or ENTIRELY DIFFERENT because it's half a millimeter wider. For Aunt Cindy, it goes in her Baked Mostaccioli (page 43) and Lasagna (page 55), the rest waiting and ready in the fridge for any last-minute saucing needs.

6 tbsp [85 g] unsalted butter

6 tbsp [90 ml] extra-virgin olive oil

1 cup [140 g] finely chopped carrot

1 cup [120 g] finely chopped celery stalk

1 cup [140 g] finely chopped yellow onion

2 lb [910 g] ground beef

2 lb [910 g] ground pork

2 tbsp kosher salt, plus more as needed

2 tsp freshly ground black pepper, plus more as needed

1 cup [240 ml] dry white wine

Two 24 oz [710 ml each] jars tomato passata (a.k.a. strained tomato purée)

¼ cup [60 g] tomato paste

NOTE: To pay homage to the Italian women in my family and their cauldrons, and because a big batch takes about the same amount of time and effort, the ragù recipe here makes enough to drown a goat. Cut the recipe in half if you want less.

In a large pot over medium heat, warm the butter and olive oil until the butter melts and bubbles. Add the carrot, celery, and onion and cook, stirring frequently, until softened slightly, 5 to 7 minutes.

Increase the heat to medium-high, then add the beef, pork, the 2 tbsp of salt, and the 2 tsp of pepper. Cook, stirring and breaking up the meat clumps, until the meat is fully cooked (no more pink) and lightly browned in spots, and any moisture that the meat released has evaporated, about 25 minutes.

Add the wine and let it bubble away, stirring and scraping up any brown bits from the bottom of the pot, until it's almost gone (and, as Elena says, until you no longer smell the wine), 1 to 2 minutes. Add the tomato passata and paste, season with a healthy pinch of salt and a few grinds of pepper, if you'd like, and let it come to a simmer.

Partially cover the pot, lower the heat to cook at a very gentle simmer, and let it slowly bubble away, stirring and tweaking the heat occasionally, until the ragù has thickened slightly and the flavors come together, 1½ to 2 hours.

Turn off the heat and keep it warm to use right away, or you can let it cool and store for up to 5 days in the fridge or 6 months in the freezer.

How to Conduct Yourself at an Italian Dinner

A meal with an Italian family can be an overwhelming experience for the uninitiated. If you're Jewish or Greek or Puerto Rican, you'll recognize the loudness, the warmth, the heaps of good food, the histrionic aunt who still smokes. But if you're not, you need to know what to expect and how to conduct yourself.

I remember my friend Chuck once joined us for dinner at Fellini's, a Chicago 'burbs restaurant—really the only one we ever went to. Chuck is just a normal white. You know, not Italian, not Jewish, just sort of miscellaneously pasty. So, he's sitting at the table and the mayhem that is eighteen members of my family is going on all around him, and Chuck looks like a passenger on the Titanic who's just realized there's no lifeboat. The fear in his eyes! Don't be Chuck.

1. First understand you're not ordering for yourself. While technically the waiter asked what you wanted and you replied, you're not actually ordering for yourself but rather for the table. The food is communal, all of it. You'll be eating off everyone else's plate and they'll be eating off yours. Advanced interlopers can attempt to negotiate—"I'll get the veal parm if you order the braciole"—but there will absolutely not be any, "I'll *also* have the chicken piccata."

2. Moreover, if someone offers you a bite, you must accept. It's not actually an offer. It's them saying, are we doing this? Are you interested in joining us on our level? So go with the flow, whether or not you feel like being fed linguine with clams by an elderly Italian woman.

3. Do not sit there quietly; that's considered highly suspicious behavior. It confuses and concerns us. It feels the way I did as a kid when I went to my mayonnaise-white friend Mark's house for dinner and only one person spoke, quietly, at a time. It was terrifying. You must be engaged in at least one loud conversation, even if it feels strange. Bonus points if it's an argument.

4. Get ready to multitask. I said "at least one conversation" in the previous point, because typically you will be juggling multiple conversations, each with many digressions. You'll need to be about to talk to your aunt Cindy about how so-and-so's cousin's wife is a real bitch while listening to your uncle Mike talk about how he noticed that an elderly gentleman in the neighborhood hasn't driven his brand-new Buick for quite a while, so you'll have to interrupt Cindy to yell across the table at your sister Kate, so she'll chime in and make fun of Mike for being obsessed with Buicks. You can train yourself by simultaneously turning on *Housewives* on your TV, playing some YouTube stand-up on your computer, and opening TikTok on your phone. Do your reps, people!

5. Inevitably the manager will come over to tell all of you to please keep it down. Do not be alarmed. He will be back at least three more times before anyone at your table even notices.

Good Luck!

Aunt Cindy's
Baked
Mostaccioli

SERVES ABOUT 10

The way my Aunt Cindy sounds when she says she'll bring baked mostaccioli when she comes over is the way I sound when I say I'll grab a bottle of wine.

Like she has to run a minor errand, or she's offered to throw together PB&Js for lunch. And then she just shows up to someone's birthday party or communion with a twenty-five-pound aluminum tray of the most delicious thing you've ever eaten.

We all call it mostaccioli, which as far as I know is the name of a southern Italian cookie and also the word Midwesterners use for tubular pasta—probably to torture non-Italians (she's a mouthful, your average Chicago mom!). It's basically baked ziti—a meaty ragù, pasta, and cheese (ricotta, mozzarella, Parmigiano-Reggiano) baked until molten. Aunt Cindy uses penne or ziti with ridges, which hold the sauce better and generally make the dish more fun to eat.

It's simple but frequently ruined by cooks who serve versions with mushy pasta or that are as dry as chalk. Aunt Cindy would never.

A handful of kosher salt, plus 2 tsp

1 lb [455 g] dried ziti rigati or penne rigate

4 cups [945 ml] Family Meat Sauce (page 37), or Aunt Cindy's (maybe she'll send *you* the damn recipe), warm

1 lb [455 g] whole-milk ricotta

1 large egg

Pinch ground nutmeg

Freshly ground black pepper

1 cup [100 g] finely grated (on a box grater) Parmigiano-Reggiano

One 8 oz [230 g] ball fresh mozzarella, coarsely grated

Preheat the oven to 400°F [200°C].

Bring a large pot of water to a boil, then add the handful of salt and add the ziti rigati. Set a timer for 2 minutes less than the time the package tells you the pasta needs to be al dente and cook it, stirring occasionally. When the timer goes off, with a colander, drain the pasta, transfer the pasta back to the empty pot, and stir in 3 cups [705 ml] of the ragù to coat the pasta well.

In a medium mixing bowl, stir together the ricotta, egg, nutmeg, pepper, and the 2 tsp of salt.

Spoon about 1 cup [240 ml] of the ragù into a 9 by 13 in [23 cm by 33 cm] baking dish. Layer half the pasta over the ragù, sprinkle with half of the Parmigiano-Reggiano, half of the mozzarella, and dollops of about half the ricotta mix. Layer the remaining pasta, then the remaining Parmigiano-Reggiano, mozzarella, and ricotta mix.

Cover with aluminum foil, and bake until bubbling at the edges, about 25 minutes. Let it cool for a good 15 minutes before you dig in.

Penne
alla Vodka

This is a very controversial pasta dish.

Like fettuccine alfredo, you can basically get it anywhere in the United States, but in Italy it's as rare as a straight Disney villain. Still, it may very well be an Italian dish—in his 1974 memoir, the actor Ugo Tognazzi included the first recipe for a vodka-spiked tomato sauce in print, but Oprah only knows who first added the cream—that took off in the kinds of American restaurants where you can get chicken parm on your pasta.

Controversial though it may be, the dish tastes really good. My version has pancetta and onion, a good dose of vodka (you don't really taste it, but it does make everything else in the dish taste even better), tomato, and enough cream to turn the whole thing penne-alla-vodka pink.

Now I'm going to introduce a new controversy: the penne part. Not only is penne on my list of pasta shapes that need to mind their own business, but it's also impossible for me to order in Italy because the pronunciation is indistinguishable from the Italian word for penis (pene). I'm gay enough already. I can't be frolicking around Italy asking for cock pasta.

1 tbsp extra-virgin olive oil

3 oz pancetta, cut into 1 in [2.5 cm] long, ¼ in [6 mm] wide strips

½ cup [70 g] diced white onion

3 tbsp vodka

1½ cups [360 ml] tomato passata (a.k.a. strained tomato purée)

A pinch of kosher salt, plus a handful for the pasta water

¼ cup [60 ml] heavy cream

8 oz [230 g] dried penne or a better tubular pasta

Finely grated Parmigiano-Reggiano, for garnish

Bring a large pot of water to a boil.

In a large pan over medium heat, warm the olive oil for about 1 minute, then add the pancetta and onion. Let it cook, stirring occasionally, until the onion is translucent, about 3 minutes. Add the vodka and cook until it has mostly evaporated, a few minutes, then keep cooking until the pancetta just starts to get crispy, about 3 minutes more.

Stir in the tomato and a pinch of salt, let the sauce come to a simmer, then partially cover the pan. Let it cook at a gentle bubble until all the flavors are well acquainted, about 10 minutes. Stir in the cream.

Once the water's boiling, add the handful of salt and then the penne. Set a timer for 2 minutes less than the time the package tells you the pasta needs to be al dente and cook it, stirring occasionally.

When the timer goes off, scoop out about 1 cup [240 ml] of the magical pasta water and set that aside. With a colander, drain the pasta, transfer the pasta to the pan with the sauce, and add about ½ cup [120 ml] of the pasta water. Over medium-low heat, cook, stirring frequently and gradually adding pasta water by the tablespoon if the sauce is looking too thick, until the pasta is al dente, about 2 to 3 minutes. Season with salt.

It's done but it's basically lava at this point, so let it cool for 48 hours (ok, a few minutes) before you sprinkle on some grated Parmigiano-Reggiano and dig in.

Cotoletta

SERVES 4 TO 6

Oh my god, I used to LOVE when my mom made Cotoletta.

(Say it with me: "co-to-let-ta"; just imagine Mario pronouncing the word "cutlet.") It's chicken but fun. But it's not chicken fingers—it's adult-kid food—everyone likes it.

She'd make cutlets for weeknight dinners because they're so easy, and it'd be me, my brother, and sister gathered around a heap of them, fighting like dogs for the crispiest piece. And they're what I'd eat on those Christmas Eves when my family did the Feast of the Seven Fishes and cooked so much seafood, even a shark would say, *OK, this is a bit much.* I don't do creatures that can't breathe oxygen ever since I ate octopus in 2017 and my dinner companion took one look at my rapidly swelling face and said, "Violet, you're turning violet, Violet." So nowadays it's me, a full-grown adult with hair transplants, and a bunch of actual children at the kid's table fighting over crispy, buttery cutlets.

We eat Cotoletta alongside pasta—in red sauce, sure, but for some reason my mom usually served them with her famous creation, Pasta della Mamma (page 34)—but you can eat them with anything. Plain. With arugula on the side. Some people squeeze lemon on top, though for me, this ruins the flavor. I say, bring on the scurvy.

¾ cup [105 g] all-purpose flour

3 large eggs

1 cup [140 g] seasoned Italian bread crumbs

½ cup [50 g] finely grated (on a box grater) Parmigiano-Reggiano

¼ cup [10 g] finely chopped flat-leaf parsley

4 medium boneless skinless chicken breasts (about 1½ lb [680 g] total)

¾ cup [175 ml] extra-virgin olive oil

4 tbsp [60 g] unsalted butter

Kosher salt, for sprinkling

Freshly ground black pepper, for sprinkling

To three separate shallow bowls, add the flour, eggs, and bread crumbs. Beat the egg well with a fork. This is all basically to glue the bread crumbs to the chicken. Add the Parmigiano-Reggiano and parsley to the bowl of bread crumbs and stir well.

Put the chicken breasts on a cutting board, and ok, wait, let's acknowledge that they look disgusting right now. As a kid I thought if you touched raw chicken, you'd get salmonella and die. Like, one touch—gone. So, wash your hands like a million times.

One by one, cover the chicken cutlets with a piece of plastic wrap and pound the living shit out of them with a small saucepan (or one of the meat hammer thingies, I guess) until they're an even ¼ in [6 mm] to ½ in [12 mm] thick. You'll feel like my mother. I wonder if she was pretending those cutlets were us kids.

One by one, coat the cutlets in the flour, then dip them in the egg, then coat them in the bread crumb mixture, pressing so they stick. It's a little messy, or at least it is when I do it. Pasta Queen, look away, this is humiliating.

In a large pan over medium heat, warm the olive oil and butter (oil for the heat, butter for the flavor, as the Barefoot Contessa says), let the butter melt and sputter, then cook the cutlets, two at a time, until crispy and a beautiful golden brown color on both sides, 4 to 5 minutes per side.

Drain on a paper towel–lined rack set in a baking sheet and sprinkle right away with salt and pepper. Keep them in a warm place, like a super-low oven, while you cook the remaining cutlets.

Kate's Meatballs

Because we're Italian, basically everyone in my family makes meatballs.

But no one is as arrogant about their meatballs as my sister, Kate. Like, she refuses to order meatballs at restaurants. She's *that* sure hers are better. And tbh, she's right.

I've never had meatballs so light and delicate—they're like little clouds . . . of meat, if that's possible. To make them that way, she skips the typical bread crumbs and instead goes for a lot of fresh bread. (She uses the squishy insides of her own homemade bread, because she's extra like that, which you'd know if you saw the claws she calls nails.) She adds milk and scrunches it altogether to make a hideous bread soup, also known as panade.

From there, the key is tenderness—tenderly mixing in the meat and other stuff, tenderly making the balls (the mixture is so loose that she uses a cookie scoop rather than rolling by hand), and cooking them, undisturbed, in the oven. The woman doesn't even finish them in the sauce because they'd fall apart. Instead, she ladles it on just before serving.

Extra-virgin olive oil

7 cups [200 g] torn-up crustless bread (into roughly 1 in [2.5 cm] pieces)

2 cups [475 ml] whole milk

¼ cup [5 g] loosely packed chopped basil leaves

1 cup [100 g] finely grated (on a box grater) Pecorino Romano cheese

½ cup [50 g] finely grated (on a box grater) Parmigiano-Reggiano

2 large eggs, lightly beaten

1 lb [455 g] ground beef

1 lb [455 g] ground pork

1 lb [455 g] ground veal

2 tbsp kosher salt

About 6 cups [1.4 L] your favorite tomato sauce or sauce from my Pasta al Pomodoro (page 155), heated

Preheat the oven to 350°F [180°C]. Grab a large baking sheet, at least 18 by 13 in [46 by 33 cm] and coat the bottom generously with olive oil.

In a large mixing bowl, combine the bread, milk, and basil and let the bread soak for a few minutes. Get your hands in there to start mixing and gently squishing to break up the bread slightly. You want it nice and soggy. Add the cheeses and use your hands to give it all a good stir. Add the eggs and stir well.

Season each hunk of ground meat on both sides with the salt, like you were seasoning a steak. With your hands, loosely break up the meats as you add them to the bowl with the bread mixture, then start mixing, gently breaking up the meat and distributing all the ingredients evenly. The result will be looser than your average meatball mixture. We're not making hamburgers.

Check the seasoning by cooking up a spoonful of the mixture in a small pan with a splash of oil. Does the mixture need more salt? OK, then add more salt! Just mix it in gently with your hands. The less you mess with the mixture, the more tender the finished meatballs will be.

Now form your meatballs one at a time and add them to the oiled baking sheet, lining them up like little soldiers. Because the mixture is so soft, my sister, Kate, uses a small cookie scoop to make the balls but you can use a spoon or your hands and form a ball as best you can. Shoot for meatballs that are a little bigger than golf balls.

Pop the sheet in the oven and bake, without messing with them, until they're cooked through (just cut one in half and look), 25 to 30 minutes.

Drain off the fat, then transfer them to a serving platter and ladle on the sauce. You might have to chisel the meatballs off the pan with a spatula or metal spoon. Any sticky, fatty bits stuck to the pan? A treat for you, the cook.

Lasagna

SERVES 6 TO 8

What I like about the Barefoot Contessa is how unrelatable she is.

She's always using stocks that she has simmered for three hours or telling us about how she and Jeffrey just bought a new boat, and immediately she has lost 90 percent of her audience. But she'll never lose me, and I've never even been on a boat. In the same way, when Ina makes lasagna, I feel like she does it in her one-thousand-square-foot kitchen with that voice of hers and for a second you think, I too can whip up lasagna on a Wednesday night without breaking a sweat. Well, you can't.

Jeanette Pamaro gets it. That's my nonna. She'd make her southern Italian American–style lasagna once a year for Christmas, with her signature pinch of cinnamon in the ricotta mixture, which is either a vestige of ancient Neapolitan cooking or a Chicago grandma's impromptu sub for nutmeg. It is the greatest lasagna. It's also a true pain in the ass. The fiddly sheets of pasta, the layering. It's like baked ziti for masochists. Making lasagna, now that my grandma no longer does, is the closest I'll ever come to manual labor. It's like I'm laying brick. Still, the sweat and tears pay off. If I can make it in my tiny kitchen, you can make it in yours.

A handful kosher salt, plus 1 tsp

12 oz [340 g] dried lasagne

1 lb [455 g] whole-milk ricotta, preferably Kate's Ricotta (page 57)

1 large egg, lightly beaten

¾ cup [75 g] finely grated (on a box grater) Parmigiano-Reggiano

Freshly ground black pepper

Big pinch ground nutmeg or a small pinch ground cinnamon

10 oz [285 g] package frozen spinach, thawed

Olive oil

6 cups [1.4 L] Family Meat Sauce (page 37), warm

One 8 oz [230 g] ball fresh mozzarella, coarsely grated

Bring a large pot of water to a boil, add the handful of salt and then your lasagne. Gently stir to prevent them from sticking to each other. Set a timer for 2 minutes less than the time the package tells you the pasta needs to be al dente, and cook, stirring occasionally.

Meanwhile, in a medium mixing bowl, combine the ricotta, egg, ½ cup [50 g] of the Parmigiano-Reggiano, the 1 tsp of salt, a few grinds of pepper, and the nutmeg. Take the spinach and squeeze the shit out of it over the sink, to drain the excess water. Chop it up, then add it to the bowl, and stir well.

When the timer goes off, with a colander, drain the lasagne well. What I do is drizzle them with a little oil and use tongs to transfer them to a large baking sheet in a single layer to cool slightly, otherwise you'll scald your hands trying to unstick them, and no one wants to eat a lasagna cooked by someone who looks like they have leprosy.

Preheat the oven to 400°F [200°C]. In a deep 9 by 13 in [23 cm by 33 cm] baking dish, ladle about 1½ cups [360 ml] of sauce. Add a layer of lasagne, a third of the ricotta mixture in dollops (spreading them out as best you can over the lasagne), 1½ cups [360 ml] of sauce, and a third of the mozzarella. Repeat the layers, ending with the mozzarella. Sprinkle on the remaining ¼ cup [10 g] of Parmigiano-Reggiano.

Cover tightly with foil and bake until bubbling around the edges, about 25 minutes. Let cool until it's no longer molten lava, about 15 minutes, before serving.

Kate's Ricotta

MAKES ABOUT 1½ CUPS [360 G] (IT'S EASILY DOUBLED)

Yes, of course my sister Kate makes her own ricotta.

She also makes her own bread and can shoot, skin, and butcher a deer, since she used to go hunting with our dad while I insisted on staying home with our mom and baking (sign #234 that I was a homosexual). Not that you need to be a seasoned killer to make ricotta. In fact, it's super easy.

Ricotta just means "recooked" in Italian, because people would cook milk or cream to separate the curds from the whey, and then recook the whey, which still had some curds left to give. We use cream, because this is the future, honey, and we're not living on a farm.

3 tbsp distilled white vinegar

2 tbsp freshly squeezed lemon juice

7 cups [1.7 L] whole milk

1 cup [240 ml] cream

1 tbsp kosher salt

Line a colander with two layers of cheesecloth, leaving plenty of overhang, and put that in the sink. Combine the vinegar and lemon juice in a small bowl, stir, and set aside.

In a medium pot, add the milk and cream, then heat over medium-high, stirring occasionally. If you're my sister Kate and you own a thermometer, wait until the mixture is at 190°F [88°C]. Otherwise watch carefully for steam and tiny little bubbles to form at the edges, 12 to 14 minutes.

Turn off the heat, add the salt and about half the vinegar mixture, and give it a gentle 10-second stir. Cover the pot and let it hang out for 20 minutes. Add the remaining vinegar mixture, give it another gentle stir, then cover and let it sit about 2 minutes more.

Dump it into the prepared colander. And yes, you're wasting the liquid a.k.a. the whey, but seriously, what are you going to do with whey? What are you, my great grandmother? And yes, it looks like you accidentally made cottage cheese soup, but be patient. Don't do anything. Just let it drain until it's as creamy as you want it—8 minutes and it's perfect for spreading on bread, 20 minutes and it's firm enough to use in your ravioli.

Actually, I love what my sister Kate does. She gathers the edges of the cheesecloth around the ricotta, twists them, and ties it to her faucet like it's a hobo stick, so the bag hangs over the sink. If you must, give it a very gentle squeeze to speed up the draining.

The ricotta keeps in the fridge in an airtight container for up to 3 days.

Uncle Mike

Stories that embarrassed a family member were go-to topics of conversation. Often at Uncle Mike's expense. As kids, we thought he was in charge. Prior to being a cop, he had been in the Marines, and before breakfast he'd call us all to the kitchen with a "Front and center!" and we'd all line up like the kids from *The Sound of Music*. When we got a bit older, we realized Aunt Cindy ruled the house, and that's when Uncle Mike became a target.

His main problem was that he was so goddamn nice. Just a sweet Irishman in a family full of jackals. My god, was this man thrifty. When it snowed, which it does all the time because it's Chicago, we'd all have to chip in to kick his driveway clear, because he refused to replace his ancient broken shovels. Whenever he told us about a new purchase, we'd sing "Cheap, cheap, cheap" like that song from *The Music Man*, and really the only thing he'd buy were Buicks. This man was sopping wet for low-mileage Buicks. He didn't even drive them. He just parked and reparked them in his driveway, rearranging them like Tetris blocks to show off for the neighbors. When my Irish grandma died, we were all over at Mike and Cindy's, and Mike comes up to me and goes, "Matt-chew,"–that's what Mike calls me–"I'm sorry to hear about the passing of your grandma." And I knew where this was going, because my grandma had a barely used Buick, so I was just waiting for it. "Matt, I'm just wondering . . . who's getting the Buick?" And we were all like, "Well, not you!"

Another major purchase was a brand-new driveway. For years, he had this twisted slab of concrete that looked like it had been bombed, which I think he secretly loved because he was obsessed with watching World War II content on the History Channel. Then one day, he got it fixed and he was obsessed. He'd just watch it all day. He'd water it, rinsing it with a hose as if nature can't handle washing dust off a driveway in suburban Chicago, then he'd watch it dry, proud like a farmer.

He was a cop, but he perceived himself as an entrepreneur, and always came to me with half-baked money-making ventures. I went to art school, so he brought me all his creative ideas, including the T-shirt with a picture of a man on his porch holding a shotgun that said, "Homeland Security." One day he cornered me in the kitchen to announce his latest: gay greeting cards! And I heard my aunt Cindy yelling from the other room, "What'll it say, 'Happy birthday from a gay'?" And he's like, "No, please, Cindy!" I broke it to him that there are already gay greeting cards featuring pictures of men with their dicks out, and he stormed off, "I don't know anything about that!" Ten minutes later, he was back with a new idea for me to paint a portrait of the Obama family and sell it. And I hear Cindy chiming in, "Yeah, and if they don't like it, you can send them a card that says, 'Sorry from a gay'!"

1 lb ricotta
Serve it with salad, ~~~~ toast
and wine

Gram Gram's
Eggplant
Parmigiana

`SERVES 4`

It took me a while to come around to eggplant parm.

For a long time, I had it out for eggplant itself. I didn't like the texture. I didn't even like the look of it, which is kind of ironic.

Back when I was in college, I spent a summer at painting school in Umbria, in a tiny town called Monte Castello di Vibio (famous for the world's smallest opera theater). There were twelve of us living in an old convent. It would've made a great reality show. Between classes ending and dinner beginning, I'd hang out in the kitchen with the cook who made our daily meals. I was the only kid at school who spoke Italian, so we kept each other company. And before the end of the summer, before I'd had my last Nutella sandwich and hugged her goodbye, I sobbed for a solid ten minutes, in part because her eggplant parmigiana was so good it was like conversion therapy. It made me into an eggplant lover, possibly in more ways than one.

When I got home, I learned to make the dish from Gram Gram, who if you're wondering, is my mom's mom. Her scribbled recipe says to serve it with "salad, garlic toast, and wine," with the last word underlined twice.

Extra-virgin olive oil, for shallow
  frying

3 large eggs

¼ cup [60 ml] whole milk

1 cup [140 g] all-purpose flour

2 tsp kosher salt, plus more
  for sprinkling

1 large or 2 medium Italian eggplants
  (about 1¼ lb [570 g]), cut into ½ in
  [13 mm] slices

3 cups [710 ml] sauce from my Pasta
  al Pomodoro (page 155), warm

A few pinches of freshly ground
  black pepper

1 lb [455 g] ricotta cheese

1 lb [455 g] scamorza cheese or
  fresh mozzarella, cut into ⅛ in
  [3 mm] slices

½ cup [50 g] finely grated (on a box
  grater) Parmigiano-Reggiano

Preheat the oven to 400°F [200°C]. In a large skillet over medium-high heat, warm about ¼ in [6 mm] of olive oil until it's shimmery. Line a large platter or baking sheet with paper towels. In a large, shallow bowl, combine the eggs and milk and whisk well. In another large, shallow bowl, add the flour and 2 tsp of salt and mix well.

One by one, coat three or four eggplant slices in the egg mixture, then the flour, then add to the skillet. Fry, flipping once, until golden brown on both sides, about 5 minutes total.

As they're done, transfer the slices to the paper towels and top with more paper towels to get rid of oiliness. Repeat until you've fried them all. Work in batches so you don't crowd the oil and bring down its temperature. Top up the oil if it gets low and let it heat back up before adding the next batch.

Start layering in an 8 by 8 in [20 by 20 cm] baking dish: First goes a thin layer of the sauce, then a layer of eggplant (slightly overlapping the slices to fit the dish is just fine), then a good sprinkle of salt and pepper. Add a layer of the ricotta, scamorza, and Parmigiano-Reggiano. Repeat until you've used everything up, ending with a layer of Parmigiano-Reggiano.

Bake, uncovered, until there's bubbling around the edges and the edges begin to pull away from the baking dish, 30 to 40 minutes. Let it cool for about 10 minutes, so you're not serving eggplant soup, then serve.

Gram Gram's
Braciole

SERVES 4 TO 6

This recipe for braciole comes from my great grandma, Gram Gram. Kind of.

I mean, I recently found the recipe she wrote in her elegant and barely decipherable cursive on a sheet of steno paper, and it says things like "1 pkg. breakfast steaks" and "make regular sauce." My theory is, the better the cook, the worse the recipe. She's made braciole literally hundreds of times. For her, it's too easy to explain, like me guiding someone through their first open mic. Be funny! Do jokes!

She makes her braciole in the lovely, spare Napoletana style—without flashy stuff like bread crumbs or prosciutto. It's just thinly sliced beef rolled around a sprinkling of cheese, parsley, and pine nuts, then braised until it's so tender you can cut it with a sharp look. You know what, this version tastes pretty close to hers, so I think I managed to fill in the blanks. And thank god, because years before I discovered the recipe, with which she kindly concluded, "I hope you understand this if not call me," Gram Gram was only accessible by seance.

4 lb [1.8 kg] thinly sliced top round
steaks

A few big pinches of kosher salt

⅔ cup [65 g] finely grated (on a box
grater) Parmigiano-Reggiano

½ cup [60 g] pine nuts

¼ cup [10 g] finely chopped Italian
parsley

¼ cup [60 ml] extra-virgin olive oil

6 cups [1.4 L] sauce from my Pasta
al Pomodoro (page 155) or your
favorite red sauce

Top a steak with plastic wrap, then, with a mallet or the bottom of a heavy pan, pound the steaks one at a time on a cutting board until they're about ¼ in [6 mm] thick each. Season the steak generously with salt on both sides.

In a medium mixing bowl, stir together the Parmigiano-Reggiano, pine nuts, and parsley. Spread the mixture over the top of each piece of beef, leaving about a ½ in [13 mm] border. Carefully roll the steaks lengthwise into nice tight little logs. Gram Gram "toothpicked" each log to keep them from unrolling. You can do that, too, using two per roll—one at each end—or sure, Ina, you can use kitchen twine.

In a wide, heavy pot over medium-high heat, warm the oil to shimmering and brown the thicc beef packages in two batches to avoid crowding, flipping once, about 10 minutes per batch. You want them really deep brown, so don't rush. Transfer them to a plate when they're done, leaving the toothpicks or kitchen twine in until you serve.

Turn off the heat, then add the sauce plus ½ cup [120 ml] of water, stirring and scraping the pan with a wooden spoon. Turn the heat back on and bring the sauce to a simmer over medium heat. Nestle the beef in the sauce in a single layer, partially cover the pot, and adjust the heat to cook at a gentle simmer, flipping the rolls once, until you can cut the meat with a spoon, 2½ to 3 hours. Gradually add water while it cooks, if necessary, to keep the sauce saucy. Be sure to remove any toothpicks or kitchen twine before eating!

Kate and Matteo's
Christmas
Ravioli

SERVES 6 TO 8

Ravioli are everything.

Even when they're bad, they're still kind of good. I used to go over to friends' houses and get really excited when their parents popped open cans of Chef Boyardee for lunch. (These were clearly not Italians.) Ravioli are so much fun that I loved the dish even when the sauce was bright orange and the pasta cooked to absolute hell.

Ravioli are like a pasta piñata—pretty on the outside and a party on the inside. You can fill them with so many things (the name of my next book)—pumpkin purée, shredded braised short ribs, ricotta and spinach, gorgeous runny egg yolks. You can sauce the parcels with anything—butter sauce, cream sauce, red sauce, meat sauce. At home, I'm almost always making cheese ravioli tossed with sage-spiked butter. That's what my sister and I make for Christmas Eve, clawing each other's eyes out over the details—THAT'S NOT ENOUGH PECORINO. YES, IT IS! NO, IT'S NOT! It ends up great every time.

She handles the filling—she makes fresh ricotta (and you can, too—see page 57). I make the pasta dough and crank it out into super-thin sheets. She points out that I made an enormous mess, which, fine, but that's easy to say when all you're doing is making the filling, KATE.

RAVIOLI

1 lb [455 g] whole-milk ricotta, preferably Kate's Ricotta (page 57)

1 large egg, lightly beaten

½ cup [50 g] finely grated (on a boxer grater) Pecorino Romano or Parmigiano-Reggiano

¼ cup [5 g] fresh basil leaves, torn by hand into small pieces

1 tsp kosher salt

Freshly ground black pepper

Homemade Pasta (page 164)

TO SERVE

½ cup [113 g] unsalted butter, cut into several pieces

12 fresh sage leaves

½ cup [50 g] finely grated (on a box grater) Pecorino Romano or Parmigiano-Reggiano, plus more for sprinkling

To make the ravioli: In a medium bowl, stir together the ricotta, egg, Pecorino Romano, basil, salt, and pepper. Cover and set aside in the fridge while you roll out the pasta.

Cut each sheet of pasta dough in half lengthwise. To the center of 4 of the pasta sheets, add 1-heaping-teaspoon dollops of the ricotta filling, starting about an inch from one of the short edges and leaving about 1 in [2.5 cm] of space between each dollop. Dip a fingertip in water and use it to moisten the edges of the pasta around the filling.

Lay the other 4 sheets over the filling so the edges more or less line up, then gently press on all sides of the filling to force out any air. Use a rotary pasta cutter or a ravioli stamp maker or a ravioli rolling pin—yes, these all exist, and you can also use an overturned cup!—to separate them into individual ravioli and repeat with the remaining filling and sheets. You'll have some scraps leftover. Just deal with it.

At this point, you can freeze as much of the ravioli as you'd like. Put them in a single layer on a baking sheet lined with parchment paper and freeze, uncovered, until hard. Then transfer to resealable bags and freeze for up to 1 month.

To serve the ravioli: In a very wide pan set over low heat, combine the butter and sage leaves and cook until the butter melts and froths. Turn off the heat.

Bring a large pot of water to a boil, add the handful of salt and then your ravioli. Cook, stirring very gently occasionally, until they're cooked (taste one!), about 3 minutes. Turn off the heat and use a spider strainer to carefully transfer the ravioli to the pan with the sage butter. Add the Pecorino Romano and gently toss.

Serve in bowls and sprinkle with more cheese.

Polenta

We Italians don't typically measure, so I was shocked when my sister, Kate, told me she had a real recipe, with amounts and everything, for the polenta we make at Christmas and occasionally throughout the year.

I don't know why we didn't make it more often—probably because pasta always won the day, and you can't serve polenta and pasta. At least, my trainer advises against it.

All I had to do was offer to fund a few months of Sculptra, and she sent the recipe right over. And until she sent it, I swear I had forgotten the secret was just a throuple of cheese, including mascarpone and both Parmigiano-Reggiano and Pecorino Romano (for the right balance of salt, umami, and tangy sharpness). There's butter, too—oh my god, my trainer's going to kill me.

5 cups [1.2 L] unsalted chicken stock
or water

2 tbsp extra-virgin olive oil

1 cup [160 g] instant polenta

1 cup [100 g] finely grated (on a box
grater) Parmigiano-Reggiano

1 cup [100 g] finely grated (on a box
grater) Pecorino Romano

1 cup [240 g] mascarpone, at room
temperature

3 tbsp unsalted butter

½ tsp kosher salt

NOTE: Using water or
boxed stock is fine, but—
and look at me like I'm the
Barefoot Contessa—it's
even better when you've
made the stock yourself.

In a medium pot over high heat, bring the stock and oil to a boil. Start whisking as you pour in the polenta in a steady stream.

Return the mixture to a simmer, then lower the heat to medium-low. Cook, stirring frequently and occasionally scraping the pot so nothing sticks, until the polenta is thick and bits of the dried corn in it are tender and eating them no longer makes you feel like a pigeon scavenging for food on the C-train platform, 5 to 10 minutes.

Add the Parmigiano-Reggiano, Pecorino Romano, mascarpone, butter, and salt, and stir until completely melted. Turn off the heat, season with salt, and serve immediately with any saucy or stewy Italian dish or spoon on some Family Meat Sauce (page 37).

Big Salad

with Gram Gram's Dressing and Cherie's Croutons

SERVES 4 TO 6

If I'm being honest, I'm not a vegetable person.

I won't *not* eat Roman-style artichokes, because I'm not a monster, and I will definitely eat the zucchini blossoms at Zi'Umberto in Rome, because they're filled with mozzarella and fried. For the most part, though, I stick to pasta. So, if there's a salad on the table, you can have it. With one exception: when my mom makes one with crisp lettuce, slightly sweet Italian dressing (passed down from her mom a.k.a. "Gram Gram"), and her own golden, garlicky croutons. OK, the croutons are my favorite part, and my poor mom can barely get them in the salad before I eat them all.

One large head iceberg, or any lettuce, really, trimmed and chopped (about 12 cups [200 g])

1 lb [455 g] Roma tomatoes, cut into wedges

½ cup [70 g] thinly sliced red onion

1 cup [240 ml] Gram Gram's Italian Dressing (page 77), or store-bought

3 cups [120 g] Cherie's Croutons (page 77), or store-bought

In a big serving bowl, toss together the lettuce, tomatoes, and onion. Add enough dressing to coat (about half), taste, then add more dressing if you like. Add the croutons, toss briefly, and serve.

Gram Gram's Italian Dressing

MAKES ABOUT 1½ CUPS [360 ML]

1 cup [240 ml] extra-virgin olive oil

½ cup [120 ml] red wine vinegar

1 tbsp kosher salt

2 tsp white sugar

1 tsp dried oregano

1 tsp dried parsley

Freshly ground black pepper

2 garlic cloves, halved lengthwise

Put everything in a jar, shaky shaky for about 10 seconds so everything gets mixed up, and pour over your favorite salad, leaving the garlic behind.

Cherie's Croutons

MAKES ABOUT 3 CUPS [120 G]

¼ cup [60 ml] extra-virgin olive oil

3 garlic cloves, minced with a garlic press

A few generous pinches of kosher salt

A few generous pinches of freshly ground black pepper

4 cups [120 g] 1 in [2.5 cm] cubed crustless Italian or white bread

Preheat the oven to 350°F [180°C]. In a medium mixing bowl, combine the oil, garlic, salt, and pepper and stir well. Add the bread, toss to coat well, then immediately (so the cubes don't soak up too much oil) transfer to a large baking sheet in a single layer.

Bake, tossing every 10 minutes, until the cubes are golden and crunchy all the way through, 20 to 25 minutes. Let cool before adding them to your salad.

Things in a Nonna's House

Ancestry.com, great. And 23andme, big fan. But the best way to tell if your grandmother is Italian is with this simple quiz.

+1 If her house has a living room that no one has ever been in, give yourself one point. Another point if the carpet is red and one more if you can see the vacuum lines.

+1 Give yourself a point for her glassed-in cabinet with sets of plates and glasses that have never been, and never will be, used.

+5 Give yourself five points if she has two kitchens—one on the first floor that, like the living room, has never been used, and another in the basement, at least in an Italian home in Chicago, which is where she actually cooks.

+10 Give yourself ten points if the subjects of the paintings and photography in the house are limited to Jesus, grandkids, and mall-quality scenes from Italy.

+∞ Actually, give yourself a point for every depiction of Jesus, two for every depiction of baby Jesus, and three for any of the Infant Jesus of Prague, who looks less like God's son and more like Lady Gaga. Holy water in a bottle shaped like Jesus is a multiplier—double your score.

If you have over two thousand points, congratulations, you've got yourself a nonna!

Cherie's Tiramisu

Some recipes are passed down from generation to generation.

Some seem to come from thin air, like the amazing tiramisu my mom makes. No grandma or great grandma showed her how to make the fluffy mascarpone cream or taught her to spike it with dark rum instead of the more traditional marsala. Instead, like a dutiful nineties mom, she pieced a recipe together from various newspaper clippings, barely competent Google searches (or more like Ask Jeeves), and years of trial and error. Her tiramisu is easy to make, though my god do you use a lot of bowls.

6 egg yolks, plus 5 egg whites

¾ cup [150 g] white sugar

1 lb [455 g] mascarpone cheese, at room temperature

2 cups [475 ml] heavy cream, cold

2 cups [475 ml] plus 2 tbsp strong, dark roast coffee or espresso, cooled

2 tbsp dark rum

1 tsp vanilla extract

40 ladyfingers (from one 17.6 oz [500 g] bag Balocco Savoiardi Ladyfingers)

Unsweetened cocoa powder, for dusting

Chill a large mixing bowl.

Bring a medium pot of water to a simmer. In another large mixing bowl that'll sit in the pot without touching the water, combine the egg yolks and sugar. Set the bowl in the pot and whisk constantly until the mixture turns pale yellow and looks super silky (lift the whisk and let the mixture dribble off—it's ready when the dribble stays on the surface for a few seconds like a little ribbon), about 5 minutes.

Take the mixture off the heat. Add the mascarpone and use a handheld electric mixer (or transfer to the bowl of a stand mixer) and beat on high speed until smooth, creamy, and slightly fluffy, 2 to 3 minutes.

In the chilled large mixing bowl, whip the heavy cream on high speed to stiff peaks, about 3 minutes. Add the 2 tbsp of coffee, the rum, and the vanilla and whip on medium speed just until smooth.

In another large mixing bowl (yes, I know, but trust me, it's worth it), whip the egg whites to stiff peaks. Using a rubber spatula, gently scrape the mascarpone mixture into the whipped cream and gently fold it in— you want to mix it in well without losing all that air you spent time whipping into it in the first place. Add the whipped egg whites about a cup at a time, again gently folding after each addition.

Into a medium mixing bowl, add the remaining 2 cups [475 ml] of coffee. One at a time, submerge 20 of the lady fingers for a count of two (any longer and they'll fall apart) and lay them in a 9 by 13 by 2 in [23 by 33 by 5 cm] baking dish (glass or ceramic, please) until the surface is covered in a single layer. Spread on half the mascarpone mixture in a nice even layer.

Repeat with the remaining lady fingers until the second layer is complete (you'll have ladyfingers leftover, it is what it is) and the mascarpone mixture. Add as much cocoa powder as you'd like to a fine-mesh strainer, and gently dust it over the tiramisu.

Cover and refrigerate for at least 6 hours or up to 2 days before serving.

CHAPTER 2

Rome

CITY OF GUANCIALE

You see a man walking to work wearing Gucci shoes, sweating through a tight blue suit, and smoking a hand-rolled cigarette.

He's forty-two but his hair is down to his jaw. He's rocking a fresh tan and it's January. This man is Rome.

You see a gorgeous woman teetering on Gianvito Rossi pumps holding hands with a man literally half her size and who's shaped like a perfect square—I mean, seriously, he's basically a LEGO. This couple is Rome.

You offer to cook lunch at your friend Giovanni's house. You make a cauldron of cacio e pepe and it's sweltering because there's no AC in Rome—Italians think it makes you sick; even when they have an AC, they'll only turn it on with the windows wide open—so the six straight men you're cooking for take off their shirts before setting the table. We all have a bit of wine, gorge ourselves on pasta, and then in a country where you can't legally get gay-married, in the shadow of the Vatican, me and a half dozen shirtless straight guys take a nap together. That's Rome.

You go to a famous pizzeria with an American friend, and she asks for extra cheese on her pizza. The waiter says, "No," and walks away. The next night you go to one of your favorite restaurants and try to order something that's right there on the menu and the waiter says, "No," and walks away. And somehow, it's charming. That's Rome.

Rome is strange and perfect. Full of confusing contradictions, fashionable and slightly out of touch, modern and ancient, a place with so many rules and also no rules at all. No, they won't make you anything but espresso after eleven o'clock in the morning. No, they won't serve you the meat course before the pasta course. But will they ever show up on time? Probably not. The rules feel arbitrary, at least until you've spent enough time there. Then they just make sense, and one day you're the one sweating through a tight blue suit and shaming some poor tourist from the Chicago suburbs for ordering an afternoon cappuccino. Maybe you've fallen in love with the city. Maybe it's Stockholm Syndrome. All that matters is you'll never be the same again.

Sometimes you come to Rome for the fantasy and Romans are happy to deliver, and to take your money. I had my first and only date in Italy, and his name was Giuseppe. (I mean, it's Rome. You're not getting picked up by Tom.) He picks me up on a Vespa, and I literally say out loud, "Am I Lizzie McGuire?" A few minutes later, we're flying through traffic like the Millennium Falcon through an asteroid field and *still*, he's driving with only one hand, because he's Italian so he needs at least one hand to talk. What struck me is that after we ate pasta and went back to my hotel, we didn't even have sex. I'm an American gay, and that is what we do. No, he looked at his watch, it was four in the afternoon, and he announced, "Now we take a nap." Afterwards, we woke up and made espresso. To this day, it's the best date I've ever had.

If you don't spend your days waiting in lines for the Starbucks in front of the Italian Parliament, you might meet some actual Romans, who, by the way, are nothing like the lobotomized caricatures portrayed in movies like *Eat, Pray, Queef*. Rome is a world freaking capital. Just because they have the Colosseum doesn't mean they don't have plumbing.

It's only the backdrop that's ancient, though it does have an effect on the culture. Walking down the street with my friend Claudio, who can look at a crumbling stone and tell you who was king at the time it first crumbled, I get why Romans take the time to enjoy life's little pleasures—a leisurely espresso before work, a nap with a pile of shirtless straights. When you're inundated by the distant past, by reminders that when you're dead, the world will happily step over your lifeless body and go about its business, then you just can't accept mediocre cacio e pepe.

Meanwhile, back in New York, people are climbing over each other to get to a job they hate, racing to lunch to eat a salad they hate, rushing to the gym to do a class they hate, then meeting up with friends to pound vodka sodas to forget about the day they hated. Honestly, a nap and an espresso would help.

Don't get me wrong, I love that in New York people dress like they're in the Burger King Kids' Club while in Rome everyone is dressed, not quite the same, but kind of the same. Rome is the most populous city in Italy by far, but it's nothing compared to New York. At any given time, there are more people than the entire city of Rome on the C train platform at West Fourth Street. Fewer people there to argue about the rules means a comforting cultural conformity, no matter how different they seem on the surface. That's how you have my friend Francesco, who was born in Rome from Calabrian parents, and my friend Tetzetta, who was born in Ethiopia and raised in Rome from the age of two by nuns, and my friend Elena, a transplant from Milan, and they all agree that adding butter to carbonara is a cardinal sin right up with sodomy.

Because of course all of the city's illogical logic extends to its pasta. Rome's iconic foursome—cacio e pepe, gricia, carbonara, and amatriciana—are all versions of one another. Essentially, cacio e pepe is gricia without the guanciale (the cured pork jowl that is to pancetta what my nonna is to a normal white grandma). Gricia is carbonara without the egg or amatriciana without the tomato.

Despite their similarities, they are each subject to different local ordinance. At any place worth going, you will never see amatriciana made with carbonara's spaghetti or carbonara with amatriciana's bucatini, even though both types of pasta are long and thin. Spaghetti works for gricia, too, but you know what also works for all three? An entirely different shape: mezze maniche, like stubby rigatoni. This logic makes 100 percent sense but *only* to Romans.

All three are typically made with dried pasta—remember, fresh is not better, just different—but cacio e pepe is often made with fresh tonnarelli (a sort of chubby fresh spaghetti) for reasons no one has satisfactorily explained. My take? I'm here for all of it.

If you're currently in Rome or going to Rome any time soon, close this book and start practicing your Italian so you can get yourself a table at Da Francesco or Roscioli or Hostaria Romana or one of the hundred places where they've been making these pastas for even longer than I've been gay. If not, read on to find my recipes for the four classics, plus one for the real fettuccine alfredo.

Pasta alla Carbonara

This is real carbonara—pasta coated in an impossibly creamy but very much cream-free sauce made from egg, guanciale, pepper, and pecorino.

Because I don't want Italy to cancel me, let me emphasize that it's not the *only* carbonara.

The cook's preferences and sense of flair determines the details. Some versions are more pecorino forward, some are heavier on porkiness, some have crisp nuggets of guanciale, and others have soft slivers, some use whole eggs, some only yolks.

But this is Rome. There are always rules. And outside Italy, people seem to be unaware of any of them. I mean, have you seen the video of Gordon Ramsey making carbonara with regular bacon, mushrooms, and parsley? I can't even. America isn't any better. I know as a country we've done worse, but my god, the number of times I've ordered carbonara only to be presented essentially with a bowl of Stouffer's fettuccine alfredo. I get it—when it's made well, I see why someone might mistakenly assume the creamy sauce contains actual cream. Why you see carbonara with peas or onions, however, I cannot tell you.

3 oz [85 g] guanciale, cut into 1 in
  [2.5 cm] long, ¼ in [6 mm] wide
  strips

5 large egg yolks

1¼ cups [125 g] finely grated (on a
  Microplane) Pecorino Romano

⅛ tsp freshly ground black pepper

A handful of kosher salt

8 oz [230 g] dried spaghetti, bucatini,
  or rigatoni

Fill a large pot with 3 in [7.5 cm] or so of water and bring to a boil. You're not using a lot because you want that water to become really starchy from the pasta, so it'll help thicken the sauce later.

In a large, heavy pan (no oil needed) over medium-low heat, cook the guanciale, stirring occasionally, until the strips have golden brown edges but are still chewy, 10 to 15 minutes. Using a slotted spoon, transfer to a paper towel–lined plate to drain so the strips don't get soggy, but keep that remaining fat in the pan.

While the guanciale is cooking and the water is coming up to a boil, in a large mixing bowl that'll sit in the pot but not touch the boiling water, whisk the egg yolks and Pecorino Romano until you have a thick paste.

Once the water is boiling, set the bowl with the yolk-cheese mixture in the pot and whisk constantly for 1 minute. Remove the bowl from the pot, whisk in the pepper, and set aside.

Add the salt to the boiling water and then add the spaghetti. Let the spaghetti soften slightly, then stir so the pasta doesn't stick together. Cook, stirring occasionally, until the pasta is al dente, about as long as the package instructions tell you, but the only way to tell for sure is to taste it yourself.

After about 5 minutes of cooking the pasta, scoop out about ½ cup [120 ml] of the magical pasta water. By the splash, add 3 tbsp of the pasta water to the egg mixture, whisking after each addition. This is so the eggs don't scramble when you add the hot pasta. Now, pour in the leftover guanciale fat and whisk until it's all glossy and smooth.

When the pasta is al dente, with a colander, drain the pasta well. Transfer the pasta to the bowl with the egg mixture and immediately start tossing constantly until the pasta is coated in a glossy, creamy sauce, about 1 minute. Add the guanciale and toss well, gradually adding pasta water by the tablespoon if the sauce is thicker than you'd like. Season with salt.

Serve in bowls.

Pig Jowls,
a Love Letter

Guanciale is the Roman cured pork product of choice and the lifeblood of three of the four iconic Roman pastas: carbonara, gricia, and amatriciana. It's everything and you need it in your life.

It's made from the guancia or "cheek" of a pig, though I like the word jowl, because it makes me think of a nonna with droopy skin pouches wiggling on either side of her chin(s). Whatever you call it, the fatty, fatty pork is coated with salt and a bold combination of spices and left to hang until it looks like hell and tastes like heaven. I swear it's 97 percent fat but in a good way. Don't get all stressed. This is a pasta book. Your trainer won't approve anyway.

Guanciale is so fatty, in fact, that it doesn't need lubrication (sex joke). You just pop it in a dry pan (no olive oil needed) and let it render its aromatic fat. Its cousin pancetta (cured pork belly) is saltier, but guanciale is somehow bolder. It's like a Virginia Slim versus a cigar.

In practically every other recipe you'll ever make, it doesn't matter what pork product you use. If you're making some sort of summer corn thing, use bacon, pancetta, or hot dogs for all I care. It'll be fine. But if you want gricia, which has like four ingredients, to taste like it's supposed to, use the right four ingredients. Use guanciale.

Cacio e Pepe

SERVES 2 TO 3

The hottest bitch on the market.

She seems basic, a little frumpy, the nerd in middle school. Then she takes off her glasses, and suddenly she's in the running for prom queen. And now she's everywhere, from New York to L.A. Too often, though, she's entangled with people who don't treat her right. Americans love to add ingredients to cacio e pepe that do not belong. So, take note: Do not accept any version that has butter, oil, or cream.

Cacio means cheese in the Roman dialect, and here that cheese is Pecorino Romano. Made from sheep's milk, it gives the city's famous pastas their distinctive funky, salty punch. *Pepe* is pepper, and we're going to grind and toast *a lot* of it in a dry skillet to bring out the aroma. If I had space in my kitchen, maybe I'd use a mortar and pestle instead of a pepper grinder, but I'm in New York City so there is no room for luxuries, like mortars or toasters, so, tranquillo, Italians. Just stop. It's better than my first apartment in New York, which was a tenement apartment with a bathtub in the kitchen but not in an *Architectural Digest*, "I found this bathtub that would be so unique in this kitchen" kind of way. No. That was where I washed my dishes *and* my ass for a whole year.

Aside from pepper ground however you can swing it and the pecorino, there's the pasta and some salt, and that's it. That's the dish. Actually, there's one more ingredient: the starchy water you're left with after cooking the pasta. (And hot tip: Better-quality pasta equals more starch in your water, so it's a good time to splurge.) The starchy water is what melds with the pepper and cheese to make this silky, creamy sauce that essentially turns pasta into a sheepy mac and cheese—in a good way. You can actually buy it in jars, this sauce, at places like Eataly and Trader Joe's. But you know, like, don't.

A handful of kosher salt

½ lb [230 g] dried bucatini or spaghetti

½ tsp coarsely ground black pepper

2 cups [200 g] finely grated (on a Microplane) Pecorino Romano

Fill a large pot with 3 in [7.5 cm] or so of water and bring to a boil. You're not using a lot because you want that water to become really starchy from the pasta, so it'll help thicken the sauce later.

Once the water is boiling, add the salt and then the bucatini. Let the bucatini soften slightly, then stir so the pasta doesn't stick together. Cook, stirring occasionally, until the pasta is al dente, about as long as the package instructions tell you, but the only way to tell for sure is to taste it yourself.

While the pasta cooks, add the black pepper to a large skillet. Yep, no oil, no butter. Just let the pepper toast over medium-high heat in your unlubed pan, stirring constantly, until the pepper releases its glorious perfume, 1 to 2 minutes. Transfer to a small bowl, let cool, then add the Pecorino Romano and set aside.

When the pasta is about 3 minutes away from al dente, scoop out about 1 cup [240 ml] of the magical pasta water from the pot and let it cool slightly while the pasta finishes cooking.

When the pasta is al dente, drain with a colander, giving it a few shakes. Very gradually—I'm talking no more than a couple teaspoons at a time—add about 6 tablespoons of the reserved pasta water to the cheese mixture, stirring after each addition to make a paste.

Transfer the drained pasta to a big bowl, add the cheese paste, and stir it vigorously with tongs for about 30 seconds to coat the spaghetti. Gradually stir in about ½ cup [120 ml] of the reserved pasta water, stirring well after each addition, until any little cheese clumps have melted and it's glossy and a little saucy. Season with salt.

Serve in bowls.

Pasta alla Gricia

SERVES 2 TO 3

I swear you can get pasta alla gricia anywhere in Rome.

At nonna's house, the post office, anywhere. The place you really want to get gricia, however, is at a trattoria, preferably the kind where the waitstaff are all relatives and you don't hear a word of English. That's where you'll be served a plate of elegant, spare perfection—essentially, carbonara without the eggs. Unlike carbonara, however, gricia is pretty much unheard-of outside Rome, so you're probably going to have to make it yourself.

To do it justice at home, make sure the ingredients are the right ones. And those are: guanciale—not bacon, not pancetta; Pecorino Romano that you grate on a Microplane into a fluffy Super Mario Bros. cloud, so it doesn't clump when you mix it with the pasta; and one of two shapes of dried pasta—spaghetti or mezzi rigatoni—due to logic that makes perfect sense, but only to Italians. The salty, starchy water you're left with after cooking the pasta is key, too. It's what alchemizes the porky fat and cheese into a creamy sauce.

4 oz [115 g] guanciale, cut into 1 in [2.5 cm] long, ¼ in [6 mm] wide strips

A handful of kosher salt

8 oz [230 g] dried spaghetti or mezzi rigatoni

¾ cup [75 g] finely grated (on a Microplane) Pecorino Romano

½ tsp freshly ground black pepper

Fill a large pot with 3 in [7.5 cm] or so of water and bring that to a boil. You're not using a lot because you want that water to become really starchy from the pasta, so it'll help thicken the sauce later. Thick is good. I said what I said.

In a large, heavy pan over medium-low heat, cook the guanciale, stirring occasionally, until the strips have golden brown edges but are still chewy, 10 to 15 minutes. (Trust me: Bite into fully crisp guanciale and your teeth will look like a hockey player's.) Take the pan off the heat. Correct, you're not draining that gorgeous fat.

Once the water's boiling, add the salt and then the pasta. Even though the water level is low, do not break the pasta. You're not seven. Stop it already. Just let it soften slightly, then stir so the pasta doesn't stick together.

Set a timer for 2 minutes less than the time the package tells you the pasta needs to be al dente and cook it, stirring occasionally. When the timer goes off, scoop out about 1 cup [240 ml] of that magical pasta water and set it aside. With a colander, drain the pasta, then transfer it to the pan with the guanciale along with ½ cup [120 ml] of the pasta water.

Over medium-low heat, let the pasta cook to al dente, stirring frequently and gradually adding pasta water by the splash to keep things moist, 2 to 3 minutes. Turn off the heat and wait a minute or so to let it cool off slightly. Add half the cheese and stir well, then add the rest of the cheese and the pepper, and stir well. Gradually add more pasta water, stirring after each addition, until the fat, cheese, and starchy liquid become a smooth, creamy sauce. Season with salt.

Serve in bowls.

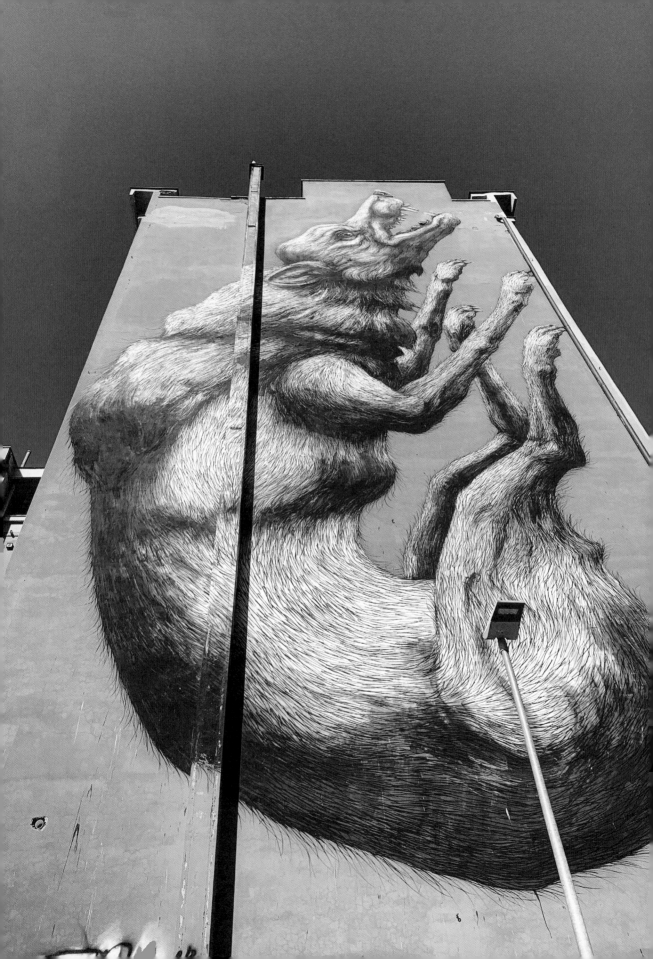

Pasta all'Amatriciana

As soon as I get to Rome, I make a reservation at Zi'Umberto.

If you're not a regular or, Oprah forbid, you don't speak Italian, approaching the maître d' to get a reservation is as intimidating as showing up to the Giants' locker room to ask for a glass of water (who am I with my sports reference). I used to arrive right at seven thirty in the evening when they opened to beg my way in until finally one day they were like, "Ciao, Matteo!" and I'm all sheepish, like "Hiyeee, sorry I just really like your food."

Dinner is at least three hours long. It begins with cacio e pepe (which is not a normal thing to order in Italy as an appetizer but whatever, they know me by now so no one even blinks) and fiori di zucca, but I ask for the gorgeous mozzarella-filled fried zucchini blossoms without the typical anchovy inside because I've held a grudge against any and all sea creatures ever since I ate octopus once and my entire body broke out in a purple blisters. Side note: What is going on with the octopus? It can change colors and shapes and escape a closed jar—even the devil is like, "Whoa."

The meal ends with baskets of biscotti being lowered from the ceiling by pulley and glasses of limoncello, which they only give you if they like you (or if you're a beautiful woman). And in the middle is the best part: the finest bucatini all'amatriciana, and my favorite plate of pasta, on the planet. And believe me, I've basically Goldilocks'd all of Rome's amatriciana. The bucatini is just the right level of al dente. The bright tomato-based sauce has just the right porkiness from the guanciale, just the right heat from chile flakes, and just the right salty wallop from Pecorino Romano.

Of course, there are endless ways to do it right. Because this is Italy, where no one agrees on the proper way to make anything. Some say there must be onions, some say there must never be wine, some say the original amatriciana didn't even have tomatoes but basically everyone agrees that now it has to.

My goal when I make it at home is the Zi'Umberto version, but will they tell me how they make it? Of course not. They won't even let my husband order chicken, even though it's right there on the menu. They're just like, *No, you'll have the rabbit.* All I can tell you is that my amatriciana is pretty close to theirs, but it's entirely possible that I just miss it so much when I'm away that I'm deluding myself.

4 oz [115 g] guanciale, cut into 1 in [2.5 cm] long, ¼ in [6 mm] wide strips

¼ cup [30 ml] dry white wine

1½ cups [360 ml] tomato passata (a.k.a. strained tomato purée)

⅛ tsp freshly ground black pepper

⅛ tsp crushed red pepper

A big pinch of kosher salt, plus a handful for the pasta water

8 oz [230 g] dried bucatini or mezzi rigatoni

Generous ½ cup [50 g] finely grated (on a Microplane) Pecorino Romano, plus extra for serving

Bring a large pot of water to a boil.

In a large, heavy pan over medium-low heat, add the guanciale and cook, stirring occasionally, until the strips have golden brown edges but are still chewy, 10 to 15 minutes. I scoop out the guanciale with a slotted spoon and transfer the strips to paper towels because I like them a little crispy, but you can also leave them be. It's up to you. Either way, keep the gorgeous fat in the pan—if it seems like a lot, that's because it is.

Add the white wine to the pan, give it a stir, and increase the heat to medium-high. Let that simmer for about 1 minute, so the alcohol evaporates and the liquid reduces slightly. Stir in the passata, black pepper, crushed red pepper, and the pinch of salt. Bring to a vigorous simmer, and let this cook, stirring frequently, until it has thickened slightly, about 3 minutes. Turn off the heat. My god, it smells like Rome!

Once the water is boiling, add the handful of salt and then the bucatini. Set a timer for 2 minutes less than the time the package tells you the pasta needs to be al dente and cook it, stirring occasionally. This downtime is when I see if anyone has texted me. No? No one loves me? Got it.

When the timer goes off, scoop out about 1 cup [240 ml] of that magical pasta water and set aside. With a colander, drain the pasta and set aside. Stir about ½ cup [120 ml] of the starchy water into the pan with the sauce (remember, those starches will help the sauce coat the pasta) and bring that back to a simmer. Lower the heat to medium-low, add the drained pasta, and cook, stirring and gradually adding pasta water by the tablespoon if the sauce is looking too thick, until the pasta is al dente, 2 to 3 minutes. Add the guanciale and Pecorino Romano and stir well.

Serve in bowls with a sprinkle of extra pecorino.

Fettuccine Alfredo

Not me going on an extended riff on stage about how fettuccine alfredo doesn't exist in Italy and starting World War III in my comments section.

There were Italians screaming that the dish isn't real and Americans shouting that it's real and it's great with shrimp. From the rubble, the truth emerged, when a restaurant called Alfredo alla Scrofa started writing on my Instagram, "We are here, we are here, we are here!" like *Horton Hears a Who!*

So obviously, my next trip to Rome included a visit and a history lesson from Tommaso, a son of the owner and the man responsible for maintaining the legacy of the original fettuccine alfredo. After Tommaso finished trauma-dumping about the American versions with chicken and cream ("Stop with this please, I beg you"), he explained the origin of the dish. In the early twentieth century, the restaurant's founder, Alfredo Di Lelio, created the dish to please his queasy pregnant wife by riffing on the classic pasta al burro e Parmigiano—pasta with butter and Parmigiano-Reggiano. Of course, if you've been paying attention, you know that the glory of an Italian pasta dish can't be captured by its list of ingredients alone.

So not only did Alfredo obsessively curate his options (sounds like me on Grindr), he invented a technique to coax out a creamy sauce (also sounds like me on Grindr) without defiling the delicate pasta. To make the real thing, you need fresh fettuccine, gorgeous sweet cream butter, and Parmigiano-Reggiano that's been aged for twenty-four months, because it's especially salty and more complex. And then you mix it all together using a spoon-and-fork choreography—which you *must* witness yourself on YouTube—so that the cheese, butter, and pasta water can merge without the pasta becoming fettuccine tartare. At home, I skip the utensil ballet and no one's the wiser.

A handful of kosher salt, plus more as needed

12 oz [340 g] Homemade fettuccine or tagliatelle (page 164) or store-bought

6 tbsp [85 g] fancy unsalted butter, at room temperature

Generous 1¾ cups [175 g] finely grated (on a Microplane) 24-month-old Parmigiano-Reggiano

Bring a large pot of water to a boil. Waiting for the water to boil is the longest part of the process—this dish is faster than the speed at which I thought my career was going to end from joking about fettuccine alfredo in the first place.

Once the water is boiling, add the salt and then the fettucine, gently stirring right away. Stand next to the pot and watch the pasta like a hawk, because fresh pasta cooks quickly. Taste a strand after 1 minute and keep tasting until just tender with a slight bite to it.

Scoop out about 1 cup [240 ml] of the magical pasta water and set aside. With a colander, drain the pasta, transfer the pasta back into the pot set over low heat, and add the butter, stirring constantly with a wooden spoon (or rubber tongs), until the butter melts. Add the Parmigiano-Reggiano, stir again, and don't freak out when it's clumpy. Just gradually add pasta water by the splash as you stir until the cheesy-butter becomes a silky, creamy sauce. Season with salt.

Now, go ahead and be a horrible American if you want and add parsley, cream, shrimp, hot dogs, ketchup, fireworks, and a flag. Otherwise, serve it as is, because it's perfect.

How to Order Coffee in Italy

In America, I'm OK with almost anyone's coffee order. I don't judge, for instance, when the woman ahead of me asks for a half-caf oat cappuccino. I don't mind—I really don't—when some guy orders a quad mocha with raccoon milk (it's sustainable!). I'm not even one of those people who hates on Starbucks. Truly, get your skinny latte with twenty-eight pumps of sugar-free vanilla. But please, for the love of god, do not do any of this in Italy.

As you are now well aware, in Italy there are rules about food and drink, and you must follow them without question. You should do this to avoid scorn, sure, but more because it's kind of the whole point of traveling: To actually be somewhere else, to embrace a moment, to experience a goddamn thing.

Here's a cheat sheet:

- You can only order three types of coffee: espresso, macchiato, and cappuccino. That's it.

- You know espresso. It's really intense, almost syrupy coffee served in the world's tiniest mug. Macchiato (which means "stained" in Italian) is just espresso with a tiny little plop of steamed milk. Cappuccino has slightly more milk. What kind of milk? Milk-milk. No 1 percent. No oat. No soy. So just stop it.

- No ice either.

- All three of these coffees are acceptable choices . . . until noon. After that, no more cappuccino. Sorry! Why? Something about too much milk being too filling. Just go with it.

- Absolutely no to-go cups. You drink, standing, at the bar of the place where you ordered. Why are we in such a rush to go somewhere with our coffee? Maybe stop your day for one second and just enjoy.

CHAPTER 3

Sicily and the South

The first time I visited Italy, when I was fifteen, I landed in the south of the country.

That's where my people come from. My nonna's family came from Naples, and her grandpa was the first to come to America. He took her to the opera, drank espresso from tiny cups, and worked for Al Capone, moving liquor in Prohibition Era Chicago. Classic.

When Nonna remarried, I got a whole new family from Sicily. Meeting my grandpa's family was one reason I tagged along with my Sicilian cousin Giovanni (in Italian, *cousin* also means friend) when he spent the summer of 2002 in Sicily.

When I landed in a shitty little airport in Catania then took a two-hour bus ride to Messina, I was skeptical of the entire country. But soon I was on the back of Giovanni's moped riding to his house, looking out at the sea with Calabria jutting up in the distance, and thinking to myself, "Dorothy, you're not on Lake Michigan anymore." I was hooked.

The next day, Giovanni took me to meet my family from Montevago, a desert town built next to the ruins of the town's first incarnation. In true Sicilian fashion, instead of reconstructing the town after the 1968 earthquake, the townsfolk left the devastation where it stood and built a new town next door. So there we were, stuffed in my uncle Calogero's tiny car and taking a Hollywood Homes tour, but instead of celebrity's mansions, it was where members of our family had died in the rubble—not exactly the beach vacation I had imagined.

There's not much for a fifteen-year-old to do in Montevago. I spent time with my Sicilian family. Most of them were in their early hundreds, so hanging out essentially meant going from house to house politely rejecting offers of ancient candies. But Messina was another story. Staying there with Giovanni provided a more appealing glimpse into my family's history. I found it on the beaches, where old men in Speedos paraded their pubes and leather-brown bellies into the Tyrrhenian Sea, emerging soon after with a sack of sea urchins, which they would shuck, suck, and toss back into the sea. I found it every time I passed a group of a dozen shirtless seventy-year-old men, smoking cigarettes while one guy butchered a swordfish and the rest bitched about their wives in the barely intelligible (to me, at least) mix of Italian and Sicilian, a language all its own. Had he stayed in Sicily, my grandpa might've been one of those men, though probably not the one chopping the swordfish. We try to keep him away from knives.

To be honest, though, what drew me to Sicily then wasn't so much discovering where I came from but grabbing me tightly to the part of my identity I felt I could be proud of rather than ashamed of. Sing it with me, Mariah: "internaliiiiiiized homophobiaaaaaa." Was it clear I was gay at fifteen? Well, a decade earlier, my aunt Cindy bought me a crystal figurine of Maleficent for my birthday, so what do you think?

On that first trip, I was far away from Betty and other nosy neighbors, and I swear no one looked at me twice. Look, just like practically every other place on Earth, Italy has certainly had its issues with homosexuality. Which is ironic, since it's home to the Vatican, where everyone thinks I'm going to hell but they're also all wearing dresses. Still, it was different in Italy than in Chicago. Like, sure, the Catholics all hated me, but then again, all the men wore Speedos. In America, I stuck out. I was "artistic," a nice way of saying "gay." In Italy, I just looked Italian. I blended in.

I went back to Messina every summer until I was twenty-one, which was when I found Rome and a whole new love affair began. And I've returned to Sicily many times since. Now that I'm an adult, I can appreciate the romance of the place with a bit more maturity than my old take, which was essentially, "Here's a gorgeous place to lay on the beach then dance all night and be super gay."

First of all, the food is out-of-control good, and I don't even do seafood, for which southern Italy is famous. In other words, I ignore the swordfish and sardines and stick to the arancini and cannoli, the pasta alla Norma and pesto trapanese. It's hard to explain to Americans, who are like OH MY GAWD I LOVE ITALIAN FOOD, and think it's all just pizza and meatballs. In fact, this tiny country is basically a thousand tinier countries stuck together, each town with its own strongly held culinary opinions and wildly different regional specialties.

Besides the food, I love that in Sicily you can see the vestiges of Greek and Arab rule, ruins that are older than the Pantheon, and Arabic influence in the language, architecture, and even the arancini (Sicily's signature rice balls). And you get to immerse yourself in island living, which is the opposite of my life in New York. When I travel to Sicily, it takes a solid week for the New York to rub off, that feeling of *Where are we going to eat, what are we going to do, what's on my Google calendar.*

Here's the Sicilian vibe in a nutshell (and since it's Sicily, that nut is definitely pistachio): Giovanni and I were on Lipari, one of the glorious little islands you can hop to, and we walked over to a busy trattoria (restaurant). We asked if we could sit, and an older woman who's clearly lived on Lipari for her whole life walked us to the one open table. As we got closer, we saw a cat dozing on one of the chairs. The woman looked at the cat, looked at us, and just said, "No." Giovanni and I were like, "What do you mean 'no'?" She gestured to the cat, and as if this explanation made all the sense in the world, as if paying customers meant nothing compared to a sleeping feline, she said, "Rocco, he's sleeping." So we left and returned to eat there the next day.

Which was fine, because in Sicily, the attitude is: Slow down. Don't worry. Everything will be fine. A hotel concierge in Sicily once explained it like this: The only unhappy people in Sicily are the ones who bring a lot of luggage. Here, you just have to take what comes.

And yes, it's become really touristy, and even more so now that the beaches are filled with gaggles of gays disembarking boats like they're Jennifer Coolidge. Giovanni is really surly about it. He's always complaining that it's harder than ever to get good cannoli or coffee granita with Sicilian brioche (which, oh my god, when it's good, is the best breakfast) and he's right. After we finally ate at Trattoria di Rocco, he went straight home to post a Google review that the food was an insult to Italians. I've seen him curse out a cafe owner for charging us five euros for a cappuccino.

In this chapter you'll find a much better pesto alla trapanese along with more of my favorite recipes from the south of Italy. Though let's be serious, if you want to actually learn something about southern Italy, Italy's islands, and honestly, Italy's everything, you'll buy my friend Katie Parla's cookbooks.

Pistachio
Pesto Pasta
with Katie Parla

How do you step on the scene decades after Marcella and Lidia corner the market on being queens of culinary Italy and immediately become one yourself?

Stop it, I don't mean me. I'm talking about Katie Parla. Her latest cookbook, *Food of the Italian Islands*, is required reading if you actually want to learn something about that special place. For the rest of you, there's me.

Katie shared the recipe for an amazing pesto, which, unlike the iconic Genovese version, hasn't been around for centuries and doesn't have so many rules about what variety of basil you can use and what material the mortar must be made from. Instead, it's a modern innovation designed to show off glorious Sicilian pistachios, the kind of dish you'd order at an upstart trattoria on the Ionian coast. It's so simple but so good that you could charge thirty dollars a plate for it at the kind of restaurant in my neighborhood where the seats are uncomfortable, the noise level is unbearably loud, and Jake Gyllenhaal is somehow always there.

Use the famous Sicilian Bronte pistachios—kidding, buy whatever they have at Whole Foods. As for the herbs, you could totally do just mint. Or basil. Or both. I don't know. See, this is why I'm not a top.

½ cup [70 g] shelled unsalted
  roasted pistachios

1 medium garlic clove

½ cup [10 g] packed basil leaves

½ cup [10 g] packed mint leaves

¼ tsp kosher salt, plus a handful
  for the pasta water

2 tbsp extra-virgin olive oil

¼ cup [25 g] finely grated (on a box
  grater) Pecorino Romano

8 oz [230 g] fusilli

Bring a large pot of water to a boil.

In a food processor, combine the pistachios, garlic, basil, mint, the ¼ tsp of salt, and about 1 tbsp of the olive oil. Pulse repeatedly to combine all the ingredients, then, with the food processor running, pour in the remaining 1 tbsp of the olive oil in a steady stream and process to a coarse paste. Transfer to a bowl and fold in the Pecorino Romano.

Once the water is boiling, add the handful of salt and then the fusilli. Stir for a few seconds so the pasta doesn't stick together. Cook, stirring occasionally, until the pasta is al dente, about as long as the package instructions tell you, but the only way to tell for sure is to taste it yourself.

Scoop out about 1 cup [240 ml] of that magical pasta water and set aside. With a colander, drain the pasta, then transfer it back to the pot over low heat. Add the pesto and ¼ cup [60 ml] of the pasta water, then toss really well to coat the pasta. Gradually add pasta water by the tablespoon if the sauce is looking too thick. Season with salt.

Serve in bowls.

Pasta alla Pesto Trapanese

Pesto is not just one thing.

The word *pesto* is just a form of the Italian verb *pestare*, which means to crush. So because this is Italian food we're talking about, of course there are a hundred different sauces made from crushed-up stuff.

To be honest, I was right there with you on the whole "pesto is pesto" thing until my first trip to Sicily, where I ordered pasta with pesto, expecting the spaghetti with green sauce I'd had in Chicago, but instead got gorgeous busiate (a twisty pasta shape local to the area) coated in pale pink sauce. This was pesto alla trapanese, I was told, pesto in the style of the city of Trapani. Made from almonds, pecorino, cherry tomatoes, and a handful of basil, the sauce is a little sweeter and brighter than the more familiar pesto genovese (see Pasta al Pesto, page 147) and unforgettably delicious. I use pine nuts—sorry, Sicilians—because almonds make my throat itch. But you do you.

Generous ¼ cup [30 g] pine nuts or
blanched almonds

1 medium garlic clove

¼ cup [5 g] packed basil leaves

¾ cup [230 g] cherry tomatoes,
halved

½ tsp kosher salt, plus a handful
for the pasta water

2 tbsp extra-virgin olive oil

¼ cup [25 g] finely grated (on a box
grater) Pecorino Romano, plus more
for serving

8 oz [230 g] dried busiate, gemelli,
or fusilli pasta

½ lemon, if your tomatoes
aren't great

Bring a large pot of water to a boil.

Meanwhile, in a food processor, combine the pine nuts and garlic, pulse a few times to get things going, then add the basil, tomatoes, ½ tsp of the salt, and 1 tbsp of the olive oil. Pulse to combine all the ingredients, then, with the food processor running, pour in the remaining 1 tbsp of olive oil in a steady stream and process to a coarse paste. Transfer to a bowl and fold in the Pecorino Romano.

When the water comes to a boil, add a handful of salt and then the pasta. Cook, stirring occasionally, until the pasta is al dente, about as long as the package instructions tell you, but the only way to tell for sure is to taste it yourself.

Scoop out about 1 cup [240 ml] of the magical pasta water and set aside. With a colander, drain the pasta, then transfer it to a large pan. Add the pesto and ¼ cup [60 ml] of the pasta water, then toss really well to coat the pasta. Gradually add pasta water by the tablespoon if the sauce is looking too thick. Squeeze in lemon juice.

Serve in bowls with a sprinkle of Pecorino Romano.

The Italian Connection

There's Italian food and there's Italian American food. And for the latter, for better or for worse, we can thank my people—no, not gays, but people like my grandparents, immigrants from Naples, Sicily, and all points south. After they arrived, the simple, poverty-fueled foods they cooked melded with the relatively hoity-toity ways of America—the land of cheap chicken, home of the brave—to create a new cuisine. In the decades since, it has morphed into a familiar roster of dishes you can probably tick off from memory. Some of these I can support. Some I cannot.

Dish: **Spaghetti and Meatballs**
Rating: **Yes, please.**

In Italy, there's pasta and there's meatballs. This red sauce classic merges what came in two separate courses onto one heaping plate. It's America, you guys—there's no time for different courses and you've gotta have meat, carbs, and veg on one plate! Well, it works. It's basically just pasta with tomato sauce and occasionally you'll take a bite of meatball.

Dish: Spaghetti Bolognese
Rating: No, thank you.

OK, this may not seem that much different than spaghetti and meatballs—I mean, it's also pasta with meat and sauce—but it is, ok? The slow-simmered sauce, born in Bologna, is so gorgeously rich and thick that serving it with spaghetti is like serving one of those heaping capicola-crammed Italian sandwiches on a cracker. For god's sake, use fresh pasta like pappardelle or tagliatelle. Or at the very least, use something sturdy, like rigatoni.

Dish: Chicken Alfredo
Rating: No, thank you.

As a guilty pleasure, I kinda love the occasional bastardized fettuccine Alfredo (see the real thing on page 104). But that's already pushing it, and adding chicken is borderline criminal. I'm saying this as someone who loved when my mom served chicken cutlets and her creamy invention Pasta della Mamma (page 34) on the same table. Enjoy your Alfredo. Enjoy your chicken. Just please don't combine them.

Dish: Chicken Parm
Rating: Yes, please.

A mash-up of Sicilian eggplant parmigiana and the crunchy chicken Cotoletta (page 49), its invention was inevitable. After all, in so many Italian American homes, there were often cutlets, and always a pot of sauce on the stove and cheese in the fridge. Now, the sandwich version I can't endorse. Bread *and* breading? What am I, twenty-four? My trainer would kill me.

Pasta
alla Norma

Who's Norma, you ask?

Well, it's one of my favorite pasta origin stories, partly because it has to do with opera, and I used to sing opera, and partly because all pasta should be named the way this one was.

Legend has it a Sicilian chef invented the pasta to celebrate the debut of *Norma*, the Sicilian composer Vincenzo Bellini's most famous opera. It's kinda like me going to Mariah Carey's Christmas concert (which I did) and pretending she wasn't two hours late (which she was) or "singing" the entire time, then creating pasta alla Mariah, which instead of cheese has glitter.

The dish is pasta with a sauce of tomatoes, eggplant, and ricotta salata that has been salted and aged so it's grateable and punchy. The key is high-quality everything—ripe summer tomatoes, gorgeous eggplant, your best olive oil—and blending the tomatoes with some of the eggplant to create a sauce with the color and creaminess of penne alla vodka.

1 small Italian eggplant (about 6 oz [170 g])

¼ cup [60 ml] extra-virgin olive oil, plus more for blending and drizzling

1 lb [455 g] tomatoes (about 4 medium), cored and roughly chopped

6 fresh basil leaves, torn at the last minute

1 garlic clove, smashed

½ tsp kosher salt, plus a handful for the pasta water

Freshly ground black pepper

8 oz [230 g] dried fusilloni, fusilli, or rigatoni

Generous ¼ cup [90 g] finely grated (on a box grater) ricotta salata

Bring a large pot of water to a boil.

Meanwhile, slice half the eggplant into ¼ in [6 mm] thick rounds and cut the remaining half into ½ in [13 mm] cubes. In a large pan over medium-high heat, warm 2 tbsp of the olive oil until it shimmers, 1 to 2 minutes. Add the eggplant, stirring the cubes and flipping the slices right away so they absorb the oil evenly, then cook in a single layer, stirring the cubes frequently and flipping the slices occasionally, until they're all softened and golden brown, 8 to 10 minutes. Transfer to a paper towel–lined plate. Wipe the pan clean.

To the pan, add the remaining 2 tbsp of olive oil, the tomatoes, basil, garlic, ½ tsp of salt, and the pepper and cook, stirring frequently, until the tomatoes have broken down completely, 8 to 10 minutes. Turn off the heat.

Once the water is boiling, add the handful of salt and then the fusilloni. Set a timer for 2 minutes less than the time the package tells you the pasta needs to be al dente.

Transfer the tomato mixture, the eggplant cubes, and a splash of olive oil to a blender and blend until smooth, adding small splashes of water if the mixture is looking too thick.

When the timer goes off, scoop out about 1 cup of that magical pasta water and set aside. With a colander, drain the pasta, giving it a few shakes, transfer the pasta back to the large pot over medium-low heat, and add the tomato mixture and ¼ cup [60 ml] of the pasta water. Cook, stirring with a wooden spoon and gradually add pasta water by the splash to keep things saucy, until the pasta is al dente and well coated in the sauce, 2 to 3 minutes. Season with salt.

Divide the pastas between bowls, top with eggplant slices, sprinkle with ricotta salata, and drizzle on a little more olive oil.

Pasta al Limone

SERVES 2 TO 3

Thick, creamy, and delicious—the original title of this book and a good description of this pasta.

The magic is in the lemon zest and juice, which brightens the whole thing up and cuts through that richness.

There are more ways to make this dish than I have hair plugs. Mine is a bit of a mash-up. It's based in part on recipes from two fellow YouTube pasta staaaaaars—Vincenzo Prosperi from Vincenzo's Plate and Nadia Caterina Munno, who goes by The Pasta Queen—and from my sister Kate.

I make mine with heavy cream and without the basil, mint, or parsley you see in some versions, so that no one could possibly call it healthy. And I like to add Parmigiano-Reggiano for some nuttiness, though to be honest I have no idea if that's traditional, and now there are probably a million Italians reading this who are furious with me. But that wouldn't be much different from how I grew up.

3 tbsp unsalted butter

2 tbsp extra-virgin olive oil

1 garlic clove, finely chopped

Finely grated zest of 1 juicy lemon, plus its juice

¼ cup plus 2 tbsp [90 ml] heavy cream

¼ cup [25 g] finely grated (on a box grater) Parmigiano-Reggiano

¼ tsp kosher salt, plus a handful for the pasta water

8 oz [230 g] dried spaghetti

Bring a large pot of water to a boil.

In a large pan over medium heat, warm the butter and olive oil. When the butter has melted, add the garlic and cook, stirring often, until the garlic is fragrant but not browned, about 2 minutes.

Add the lemon zest, give it a stir, then add the lemon juice and cook for 1 minute. Add the heavy cream and Parmigiano-Reggiano and simmer, stirring frequently, until thickened slightly, about 4 minutes. Season with ¼ tsp of the salt, turn off the heat, and set aside.

Once the water's boiling, add the handful of salt and then the spaghetti. Let the spaghetti soften slightly, then stir so the pasta doesn't stick together. Set a timer for 2 minutes less than the time the package tells you the pasta needs to be al dente and cook it, stirring occasionally.

When the timer goes off, scoop out about 1 cup [240 ml] of the magical pasta water and set aside. With a colander, drain the pasta, transfer the spaghetti to the pan of that luscious sauce over medium-low heat, and stir to coat well. Cook, stirring occasionally and gradually adding splashes of pasta water by the tablespoon to keep things creamy, until the pasta is al dente, 2 to 3 minutes. Season with salt.

Serve in bowls.

Aglio e Olio

Virtually unpronounceable to non-Italians, this deceptively simple pasta is sometimes attributed to Naples, but I attribute it to the first hungry cook who was craving pasta but had nothing in their pantry but olive oil and garlic.

That's literally what the name means—pasta with garlic and oil—and there's not much more to it besides a little parsley and chili. It's giving, *It's midnight and I just got home from the disco.*

Aglio e olio is so simple, it *seems* almost thrown together. And like so much Italian cooking, it *is* sort of thrown together—just in a very particular way. The pasta is al dente. The garlic is gently sizzled to infuse its flavor in the oil. The starchy pasta water, if you're not already tired of hearing it, is the eye of newt in this potion that turns the flavorful oil into a creamy sauce that coats each strand. The better the dried pasta, the starchier the water, the better the result.

A handful of kosher salt

8 oz [230g] dried spaghetti

¼ cup [60 ml] extra-virgin olive oil

3 garlic cloves, finely chopped

¼ tsp red pepper flakes

2 tbsp finely chopped flat-leaf parsley

Fill a large pot with 3 in [7.5 cm] or so of water and bring that to a boil. You're not using a lot, because you want that water to become really starchy from the pasta, so it'll help thicken the sauce later.

Once the water is boiling, add the salt and then the spaghetti. Even though the water level is low, do not break the pasta. Let it soften slightly, then stir. Set a timer for 2 minutes less than the time the package tells you the pasta needs to be al dente, and cook, stirring occasionally.

About 5 minutes before the timer goes off, in a large pan over medium heat, warm the olive oil. Add the garlic, let it sizzle, stirring occasionally, until fragrant but not browned, about 30 seconds. Add the red pepper flakes and cook until fragrant, 10 seconds more. Scoop out ½ cup [120 ml] of the magical pasta water and add it to the pan (stand back; it'll bubble and spit) along with the parsley. Let the mixture bubble until the timer goes off. Turn off the heat.

Scoop another 1 cup [240 ml] of pasta water and set aside. With a colander, drain the pasta, then transfer the spaghetti to the pan with the garlic mixture. Over medium heat, cook, stirring constantly and gradually adding pasta water by the splash to keep things saucy, until the oil and pasta water form a glossy, slightly creamy sauce that coats the pasta and the pasta is al dente, 2 to 3 minutes. Season with salt.

Serve in bowls.

Cherie's
Struffoli

Every Christmas, my great grandma, Gram Gram, sent us a care package full of tiny balls of fried dough, essentially little donut holes, called struffoli, or as we all called them at the time, "striffles," because as Americans we just get off butchering other languages, not just English.

Gram Gram was from Naples, which you already knew if you're also napoletano like we are, because no one from Northern Italy is making struffoli. Supposedly, it's a dish with Greek origins, which makes sense—after all, Naples was founded by the Greeks like a million years ago. They named it Neapolis, meaning New City—from the people who brought you *The Iliad* and *The Odyssey* comes the least creative city names ever.

We'd tear into the Gram Gram's package like animals. Because Gram Gram thoughtfully packed the honey on the side so the struffoli would survive the journey, we'd heat the honey up then apply it to our own specifications. My sister, Kate, liked struffoli with just the tiniest bit of honey, but I liked mine good and coated, LIKE THEY'RE SUPPOSED TO BE, KATE. Then we'd add sprinkles (those little crunchy spheres, not the stuff destined for ice cream) and go to town. Any leftovers sat on the counter for snacking. A bowl of striffles and coffee the next morning? So good.

When Gram Gram died, my mom, Kate, and I set out to crack the striffles formula, and I swear we did it. It's pretty damn simple, and freshly fried striffles have the best texture—fluffy inside with a delicately crispy exterior. Don't fear the frying process. And don't skimp on the honey, KATE.

2½ cups [350 g] all-purpose flour

½ cup [100 g] granulated sugar

1 tsp baking powder

½ tsp kosher salt

½ cup [120 ml] whole milk

2 tbsp salted butter, melted

1 tsp vanilla extract

1 large egg

Vegetable oil, for deep frying

¾ cup [230 g] honey

1 tbsp multicolored nonpareils
  (a.k.a. those tiny round sprinkles)

In a large mixing bowl, stir together the flour, sugar, baking powder, and salt. In a medium mixing bowl, whisk the milk, butter, vanilla, and egg, then dump it into the flour mixture. Mix by hand until a dough comes together, then transfer to a work surface and knead until smooth-ish, 1 to 2 minutes. Don't go at it so hard and long that it turns into rubber.

Grab about a quarter of the dough, roll it into a 1 in [2.5 cm] wide snake, then slice into ½ in [13 mm] pieces. Repeat with the rest of the dough. Now roll all those little pieces into balls and set aside on a plate or baking sheet.

You're going to deep fry—stop it, it's not hard. Line a big baking sheet with paper towels. Pour about 2 in [5 cm] of oil into a large pot over medium heat and get it hot. The recipe my mom uses says the oil should be 375°F [190°C], but come on, we're Italians, we eyeball. Test the oil by adding a piece of dough—if it bubbles like crazy, the oil is ready.

Now, add about half the balls to the oil (just hold the plate close to the oil and add them carefully—you're not trying to maim yourself just for sweets). Cook, stirring with a spider strainer the whole time, until they puff and turn golden all over and are cooked through, about 3 minutes.

Using the spider strainer, transfer the struffoli to the paper towel–lined baking sheet to drain. Snack on a few. You deserve it. Give the oil a minute to get nice and hot again, then fry the rest the same way.

The struffoli are so good warm, so get the honey going in a small saucepan over medium-high heat. Transfer the struffoli to a plate, and when the honey reaches a boil, carefully spoon as much as you want over them. Sprinkle with the nonpareils and serve.

CHAPTER 4

Found Family

GAYS

There's the family you're born with and the family you make.

Matteo   **Nick**

And in New York, for the past thirteen years, my gay family has been Bob, Monét, Patti, Jacob, Taylor, Alfredo, and Kennedy— ridiculous names, I know.

Before we were old and some of us won *RuPaul's Drag Race*, I'd finish my stand-up around ten in the evening, then Patti, Taylor, and I would go see Bob's and Monet's drag shows. Then at five in the morning we'd end up at a diner called, literally, the Flame. It turns out a diet of Red Bulls and mozzarella sticks isn't great for the skin. After a couple of months, we all got bacne.

NICK: And what's your excuse now?

MATTEO: Nick Smith, everyone. My arch nemesis, bane of my existence. I've never liked him. I was first subjected to Nick by our mutual friend Bob. So, Nick, how did you meet Bob?

NICK: I met Bob on Grindr, OK? I went over to his apartment to hook up, but we ended up spending the night watching Golden Buzzer moments from *Britain's Got Talent* and *The Voice Kids* (Philippines). And I happened to mention I didn't have any gay friends.

MATTEO: So, Bob calls us like Miss Hannigan from *Annie* to tell us he got his hands on a wayward gay orphan. Bob says, "Look, he's in his twenties and he has no gay friends. Can he just hang around?" Next thing you know, we're all at Bob's as usual but with a gayer version of Slender Man sitting on the couch. To try to get us talking, Bob mentioned that we both sang opera.

NICK: Bob thought it was something we could bond over. But in true us fashion, Matteo and I immediately started arguing. Because it turns out he loves Maria Callas and I hate Maria Callas. That was the start of our friendship.

MATTEO: Yeah, and you like Sarah Brightman. What's the opposite of bonding?

NICK: Sarah Brightman? Let's not get crazy. Also, only one of us actually sang opera.

MATTEO: Excuse me, I sang opera at Carnegie Hall.

NICK: Yeah, at the end of your "comedy show," which was so poorly conceived that you let *me* on stage to do two minutes of jokes. Meanwhile, I have a bachelor's and a master's degree in opera performance.

MATTEO: I will say that we are both bass singers and my voice goes lower than Nick's.

NICK: Oh please, how many times have you heard me sing?

MATTEO: I've heard you sing on *Fortnite*—I believe it was "God Bless America" as Liza Minelli.

NICK: Fine, his voice goes lower. Mine is prettier.

MATTEO: There we go. I'm Maria Callas. You're Beverly Sills.

NICK: I don't like you.

MATTEO: Great. Anyway. A lot of gays go out. We never go out. We all gather at someone's apartment and watch YouTube videos and argue about ridiculous things, like which of us would win *Drag Race* who hasn't already won, because it should be said that Bob is Bob the Drag Queen and Monét is Monét X Change. If you know, you know. And of course, we endlessly play *Super Smash Bros.* and *Fortnite*.

NICK: Matteo and I became really close during the pandemic, when we started playing *Fortnite*, which we've now done pretty much every day—for hours a day—for the past four years. Shockingly, Matteo and I are able to coexist on the same team. He plays as a red Stormtrooper, the Scarlet Witch, or Spiderman.

MATTEO: Nick only plays as a lady with glasses, heels, and a pencil skirt. We call her "The Secretary." And now when Nick walks into a room, I just see him in a pencil skirt and heels. Video games are how I really got to know Nick, because they reveal who people really are: Are you a team player? Anxious? Complimentary?

NICK: Exactly. That's when you found out that I'm an angelic soul. My whole life I've had a gift for making situations worse, for homing in on someone's weakness and really going in. And I learned pretty quickly that Matteo can be gullible and sensitive.

MATTEO: One night, we're at Bob's just screaming at each other for hours in *Smash*. Later, Nick is giving everyone there a very kind, formal goodbye—everyone except me. I'm the baby from a large family. When you're the youngest, you always feel left behind. So, I'm all, "Nick, stop it, say goodbye!" And he just starts the goodbyes over, skipping me again, and leaves. The next morning, Nick texts the group with personalized thank yous, everyone's name typed out but mine.

NICK: Matteo kept getting more and more upset. It was just the best.

MATTEO: I think you fall in with your crew in the same place you fell in with your family. I'm the little brother. Bob is the matriarch. Monét is the fun aunt. Patti is the red-headed middle child. Jacob is the nerdy cousin. He's basically Sailor Mercury. If you have a question, a computer will be brought out and googling will be done. Nick is the crotchety older sister or the stepdad you barely tolerate. Or the angry grandma. Think Bea Arthur's character on *The Golden Girls*. He even dresses like Dorothy. Or Maggie Smith in *Downton Abbey*.

NICK: I do enjoy dressing in pretty blouses, I'm not ashamed. Meanwhile, you dress like one of the Goonies. Just a closet full of jeans and the same T-shirts in different colors. Clothing is for Matteo what food is for me.

MATTEO: True. My Goonies attire is Nick's Chipotle burrito, which he has for lunch *every day*. And not "every day" as in "often," but every day as in the staff at the Chipotle know him because he gets one every single day.

NICK: Correct. I also enjoy Domino's, Popeye's, and Dunkin'. The food is cheap. It fills me up. I eat because otherwise I'd die. Not like Miss Michelin Star over here. For Matteo, if it's not chicken breast and brown rice for his muscles, it's got to be pasta handcrafted by an Italian man with tattoos and one of those tall white hats. He drags me to these places, and I'm not saying they're not good, but I couldn't give three less shits.

MATTEO: You truly are trash to the very soul. But it's not quite true that you don't care about food. I don't think I've ever seen him as happy as when he's stooped over a plate of lasagna fritta at Olive Garden.

NICK: That's true. It's perfect.

MATTEO: None of our friends cook either. Nick never compliments my cooking, but he does ask me to cook for him.

NICK: Excuse me, I cook, too. What about my c*m cookies?

MATTEO: Every Christmas he makes these Italian wedding cookies with ricotta.

NICK: Well, I don't use any ricotta and I don't wait for the cookies to cool down so when I pour on the icing, the cookies just look like I splooged all over them.

MATTEO: Disgusting.

NICK: You've never had them!

MATTEO: Because they look like they have c*m all over them.

NICK: Because suddenly c*m is where you draw the line.

MATTEO: I think our relationship works because we find each other funny. It's the reason our entire group works.

NICK: I'm a pessimist and a bully. So those are the type of people I gravitate toward. I ignore people I don't like. If I'm being nice to someone, then I'm only engaging with them out of obligation. If I make fun . . .

MATTEO: Say it, Nick. Come on. You do like me.

NICK: Allegedly.

NATURAL WINE
VIN NATUREL
VINO NATURA
ナチュラルワイン
VINO NATURALE
WINE BY THE BOTTLE ONLY
STOP GENOCIDE

Pasta al Pesto

SERVES 2 TO 3

We're making pasta pesto! Delicious *normal* pasta pesto (something that even someone like Nick *might* enjoy).

We're not plucking leaves of Genovese basil from our garden in Liguria. We're not working a mortar made of marble and a pestle made of wood up in here. I'm in New York, so all we have is basil from the bodega and a food processor that drowns out the sounds of the guy on my block who brings out a crappy karaoke machine every day at six in the evening and sings songs only from the seventies.

Still, it's really good, and so simple. A big handful of basil leaves buzzed with a few garlic cloves, pine nuts, olive oil, and a mixture of Parmigiano-Reggiano (for its sweet nuttiness) and Pecorino Romano (for its salty, sheepy punch). Linguine and I don't have a great relationship, but I'm throwing a bitch a bone here, because it is traditional. In Liguria, you often see it made with trofie, a fresh twisty pasta shape that's not impossible to find dried, and there are potatoes and green beans thrown in, which I like but sometimes I'm just about pasta and sauce.

147

4 cups [80 g] basil leaves

2 tbsp pine nuts

2 medium garlic cloves

¼ tsp kosher salt, plus a handful for the pasta water

½ cup [120 ml] extra-virgin olive oil

Generous ¼ cup [25 g] finely grated (on a box grater) Pecorino Romano

Generous ¼ cup [25 g] finely grated (on a box grater) Parmigiano-Reggiano, plus more for serving

8 oz [230 g] spaghetti or, fine, linguine

Bring a large pot of water to a boil.

In a food processor, combine the basil, pine nuts, garlic, and the ¼ tsp of salt. Yes, a food processor—sorry to all the irate Genovese nonnas who definitely bought a book about pasta from a gay from Arlington Heights. Pulse a few times until it's all coarsely chopped, then add about 1 tbsp of the olive oil and pulse once or twice more. Add the Pecorino Romano and Parmigiano-Reggiano, then with the food processor running, pour in the remaining 3 tbsp of olive oil in a steady stream and watch as a gorgeous, glossy paste forms.

Once the water is boiling, add the handful of salt and then the spaghetti. Let it soften slightly, then give it a stir so the pasta doesn't stick together. Cook, stirring occasionally, until the pasta is al dente, about as long as the package instructions tell you, but the only way to tell for sure is to taste it yourself.

Scoop out about 1 cup [240 ml] of the magical pasta water and set that aside. With a colander, drain the pasta, giving it a few shakes, transfer the spaghetti to a large skillet. Add the pesto and ¼ cup [60 ml] cup of the pasta water and toss really well to coat the pasta. Gradually add pasta water by the tablespoon if the sauce is looking too thick.

Serve in bowls with an extra sprinkle of Parmigiano-Reggiano.

My Pasta Idols

Bob, Nick, and Monét, I love them dearly. They love me dearly. But they do not want to hear me go on about pasta alla gricia. So, like an adult, I've sought out new friends I can go to to get my needs fulfilled.

A few years back, I was opening for Aziz Ansari (yeah, no big deal) in Rome, and he said his friend was going to take us out to dinner. For some reason I expected a cuddly "OMG spaghetti" kind of person. Instead, I got **Katie Parla**. You know what's better than cuddly? Tough, fiercely smart, and definitely cooler than you. A Roman woman in spirit who just happens to hail from New Jersey, Katie has become the go-to guide for all things Italian. Her cookbooks are everything. Remember how Rain Man could take one look at a box of spilled toothpicks and tell you immediately how many there were? That's her but with basil. And she's not telling you how many leaves but where it was grown and how to use it.

Then there's my parasocial paramour, **The Pasta Queen**. I'm obsessed. She is like . . . OK, you know how Italy doesn't have an army? I mean, they do, but they can't fight because they're too concerned about what's for dinner? Well, not since Ancient Rome has anyone seen a warrior like Nadia Caterina Munno, who parachutes into TikTok wearing vintage Gucci while cooking carbonara and looking like an Italian Sofia Vergara out to save us all from bad pasta. Her videos are everything. So are her outfits. Her cookbook is probably better than this one. Are we technically friends? No. Do we occasionally chat on Instagram and has that made me prouder than just about any other achievement in my life? Maybe.

Two Mac
and Cheeses

The camera pans to two dear friends, Nick Smith (7 feet tall, 60 pounds, shoulders like a curtain rod, wearing a pussy-bow blouse) and me, Matteo Lane (biceps, abs for days, and hair that definitely hasn't been transplanted, why do you ask?).

MATTEO *(who has mild to moderate gay voice)*
Today we're making two different macaroni and cheeses, Nick's style and then my style.

NICK *(who sounds like Squidward, but more nasal)*
Yes, the correct way and the pretentious way.

MATTEO
Nick is literally opening a box of Kraft. I'm embarrassed for him. He's picked the basic "elbow" version for some unknown reason. He's not even using spirals.

NICK
Well, I hate you, so here we are.

MATTEO

I'm making an Italian version of macaroni and cheese modeled after something I had in Italy. The Pasta Queen makes a great one with four cheeses, but I'm only using three, so please don't block me! Basically, I'm going to melt the cheeses in a mixture of butter, milk, and heavy whipping cream.

NICK

You're not whipping it though.

MATTEO

It's *called* heavy whipping cream, Nick.

NICK

So you're making cheese soup. I'll pass.

MATTEO

If a car ran you over, I would sleep so soundly.

Nick's Infamous Mac & Cheese

1 box Kraft white cheddar mac & cheese

4 tbsp [55 g] unsalted butter

¼ cup [60 ml] whole milk

Some pepper

To be read in Nick's Squidward-esque drawl. Bring a small pot of water to a boil. Open the box of mac and cheese and remove the packet of cheese powder. Now we wait.

Once the water is boiling, dump in the pasta and cook as long as the box tells you to. Dump the pasta into a colander, gleefully watching Matteo's precious pasta water go down the drain.

Add the hot pasta back to the pot and stir in the butter until it melts. Add every last granule of the cheese powder and mixy mixy. Now, you may be thinking to yourself, "This looks dry." Well, stir in the milk and it's dry no more. Add pepper, take your bow, and eat it from the pot.

Matteo's Macaroni and Cheese

1½ cups [360 ml] heavy cream

¾ cup [180 ml] whole milk

4 tbsp [55 g] unsalted butter

½ cup [85 g] coarsely grated fontina

¼ cup [50 g] coarsely crumbled gorgonzola dolce

½ cup [50 g] finely grated (on a box grater) Parmigiano-Reggiano

¼ tsp freshly ground black pepper

A pinch of ground nutmeg

A handful of kosher salt

8 oz [230 g] large shells

Bring a large pot of water to a boil.

In a large pan over medium heat, add the heavy cream, milk, and butter. Bring to a simmer, stirring frequently, then add the fontina, gorgonzola, and ¼ cup [25 g] of the Parmigiano-Reggiano. Cook, stirring, until the cheeses have melted and the sauce is smooth, about 3 minutes.

Add the pepper, nutmeg, and the remaining ¼ cup [25 g] Parmigiano-Reggiano and stir. Continue to simmer, stirring frequently, until the Parmigiano has melted and the sauce has thickened slightly, about 5 minutes. Turn off the heat and cover to keep warm.

Once the water's boiling, add the salt and then the shells. Gently stir so the pasta doesn't stick together. Cook, stirring occasionally, until the pasta is al dente, about as long as the package instructions tell you, but the only way to tell for sure is to taste it yourself.

With a colander, drain the pasta, giving it a few shakes, then transfer the pasta to the pan of cheese sauce. Toss really well to coat the pasta. Season with salt.

Serve in bowls.

Pasta
al Pomodoro

SERVES 2 TO 3 (PLUS EXTRA SAUCE)

If you want to know if an Italian place is any good, try their red sauce.

It tells you everything. If they can't make tomatoes, garlic, and olive oil taste good, my heart goes out to anyone who eats their braciole.

There's no excuse to screw it up, so don't. And if you're going to screw it up, at least screw it up yourself. Whatever you do, please don't be my friend and Prego devotee Nick. He made me pasta once and the sauce was so sweet it tasted like he'd just melted red Skittles. I mean, come on, look how simple this recipe is. You don't need to buy a jar of sauce. Why are we in such a rush to save twenty minutes when we're just going to spend them on the couch scrolling TikTok? Which reminds me, follow me @matteolane.

RED SAUCE

½ cup [120 ml] extra-virgin olive oil

10 garlic cloves, smashed then peeled

¼ tsp red pepper flakes

Two 24 oz [710 ml each] jars tomato passata (a.k.a. strained tomato purée)

1 tbsp kosher salt

1 cup [20 g] basil leaves

PASTA AL POMODORO

A handful kosher salt

8 oz [230 g] dried spaghetti

Finely grated Parmigiano-Reggiano, for serving

NOTE: A simple red sauce is a staple of every Italian American household, preferably cooked in a pot big enough to bathe in. This recipe doesn't make *that* much, but it does give you enough for a week's worth of use, from Kate's Meatballs (page 51) to Gram Gram's Braciole (page 65). It keeps frozen for up to 6 months.

To make the sauce: In a medium pot over medium heat, combine the olive oil and garlic and let it start to sizzle, about 2 minutes. Cook, stirring occasionally, until the garlic gets a little color, about 2 minutes. Stir in the red pepper flakes and cook until fragrant, about 30 seconds more.

Add the passata, the 1 tbsp of salt, and 1 cup [240 ml] of hot water. Bring to a simmer, cover, and lower the heat to cook at a nice moderate simmer, stirring occasionally, until it has thickened slightly, 20 to 25 minutes.

Scoop out and discard the garlic, then add the basil, tearing the leaves as you do. Stir to wilt the basil, season with salt, and turn off the heat. You'll have about 6 cups [1.4 L] of sauce. If you're making my pasta al pomodoro, scoop out all but about 1½ cups [360 ml] of sauce and reserve it for another time.

To make the pasta al pomodoro: Bring a large pot of water to a boil.

Once the water's boiling, add the handful of salt and then add spaghetti. Let the spaghetti soften slightly, then stir so the pasta doesn't stick together. Set a timer for 2 minutes less than the time the package tells you the pasta needs to be al dente and cook it, stirring occasionally.

When the timer goes off, scoop out about 1 cup [240 ml] of that magical pasta water and set aside. With a colander, drain the pasta, transfer the pasta to the pot of sauce over medium-low heat, and add ½ cup [120 ml] of the pasta water. Cook, stirring occasionally and gradually adding pasta water by the splash to keep things saucy, until the pasta is al dente, 2 to 3 minutes. Season with salt.

Serve in bowls sprinkled with Parmigiano-Reggiano.

Risotto
allo Zafferano

My friend Elena is everything.

She lives in Rome but she's from Milan and cooks my favorite version of her home region's risotto allo zafferano. (My god, the Italian name of the dish is so lovely when warbled by this tiny, gorgeous woman. In English, it just sounds boring: Saffron risotto.)

I'm not nearly as comfortable making risotto as I am cooking pasta, but all in all, it's not so different. Instead of really nice al dente pasta made incredible by some seasoning and starchy water, you're cooking nice al dente rice with some seasoning and coaxing out the starch from the grains so the whole thing is super creamy.

Here, those seasonings are Parmigiano-Reggiano, butter, and beef stock—even Elena says boxed is fine, but make your own or who am I kidding, buy it from one of those fancy butcher shops where they dismember whole cows once a week. And of course, the headlining ingredient: saffron, for its subtle flavor and stunning yellow color, like the sun on a plate or, and I apologize to the entire country of Italy, like Kraft mac and cheese, in the best way.

5 cups [1.2 L] unsalted beef stock or vegetable stock

¼ tsp saffron threads

3 tbsp extra-virgin olive oil

½ medium yellow onion, finely diced

1 tsp kosher salt

1½ cups [300 g] carnaroli or arborio rice

½ cup [120 ml] dry white wine

¼ cup [55 g] unsalted butter, cut into a few pieces

¼ cup [25 g] finely grated (on a box grater) Parmigiano-Reggiano

In a medium pot over medium-high heat, warm the stock just until it simmers. To a heat-proof container, add the saffron, ladle on about ½ cup [120 ml] of the hot stock, and stir well. Cover and set aside. Turn off the heat and cover the pot to keep the stock hot.

In another medium pot (a nice wide one, like a Dutch oven, is great here) over medium heat, heat the olive oil until it shimmers, then add the onion and salt, and cook, stirring occasionally, until translucent, about 5 minutes. Add the rice and use a wooden spoon to gently move the grains around to coat them in the oil and toast them. Do not attack them. They're ready when all but the center of the grains turn translucent, 1 to 2 minutes.

Add the wine and cook, stirring gently, until it's just about gone, about 2 minutes. Now, begin adding the hot stock about 1 cup at a time, and cook, gently stirring occasionally, only adding the next cupful when the previous cup has nearly been absorbed by the rice, until the rice is al dente, about 20 minutes.

You may not use all the remaining stock. Also, we're not stirring every second, like I used to hear was the key to risotto. First of all, we don't have the patience. Second, as Elena says, you'll end up smashing the rice.

Stir in the saffron liquid and cook, stirring, until it's fully absorbed and the risotto is creamy. Turn off the heat, fold in the butter and Parmigiano-Reggiano, and season with salt.

Serve in bowls.

Homemade Pasta

MAKES ABOUT 1⅓ LBS [600 G]

Remember, fresh pasta isn't better than dried.

It's different, with a slick texture and delicate chew versus the enticing bite of dried. Each type is suitable for a different array of sauces. Following the rules will not only spare you the embarrassment that comes with serving spaghetti Bolognese—an arrestable offense in parts of Italy, I'm sure—but you'll also be able to taste the reasons behind them.

And despite what you might think from all those years of hearing that nonnas who have made pasta every day for forty years make the best—OK, true, but you, too, can make fresh pasta that'll kill at the table, even the first time you try it. And no, there's no need to roll the pasta by hand like nonnas do with what looks like the handle of a broomstick. After you make the dough, kneading to work the glutens that give pasta its springy bite then letting them relax for half an hour, you'll pass the dough through a simple hand-crank pasta machine or, if you have the kitchen space and the *Great British Bake Off*-ness to own a stand mixer, a pasta-roller attachment. Both cost about as much as a plate of cacio e pepe at the Manhattan location of Roscioli. No excuses, people.

3½ cups [490 g] 00 flour, plus more for dusting

4 large eggs

1 tsp kosher salt

NOTE: 00 flour, also known as doppio zero (double zero), is an especially finely ground flour that, if you ask me, makes pasta with the best texture.

Pile the flour on a clean work surface or dump it in a large bowl. Create a well in the middle, then add the eggs and salt to the well. Using a fork, beat the eggs well. Next, start stirring in small circular motions and gradually incorporate the flour into the eggs, little by little, until it's more or less mixed in. Now get in there with your hands and stir and knead just until the flour is completely incorporated and you have a sticky, craggy dough.

Sprinkle on a little flour (or lightly flour a work surface and dump out the dough) and knead the dough— that's fold, push down with your palm, then rotate 45 degrees, and repeat—until the dough is smooth and has firmed up, about 10 minutes. This takes some elbow grease, so you can skip arm day at the gym. Give it a gentle poke with your finger. When it's ready, the dough should spring back slowly. Or as Elena says, "When you do this, she come back." God, I love her.

Cover the dough with plastic wrap or a damp cloth and let sit at room temperature for at least 30 minutes.

Cut the dough into 4 equal pieces. Use a rolling pin to roll out the pieces so they're about 1 in [2.5 cm] thick and dust lightly with flour on both sides. Cover with a kitchen towel to keep them from drying out.

Starting on the widest setting of a pasta machine—one of those hand-crank devices or an attachment to a stand mixer—feed one piece of dough through the machine, using your free hand to gently guide the flattening dough out. Fold it lengthwise, then pass it through again at the same setting. Go to the next setting and pass it through twice the same way. Now pass it through once at each setting, working your way to the narrowest one.

cont'd.

Transfer to a clean, lightly floured work surface and cover with a kitchen towel. Repeat with the remaining dough pieces. Now you're ready to make Ravioli (page 69)!

Or you can cut the dough into fresh tagliatelle or fettuccine. Dust with a little more flour, fold the sheets in half lengthwise, then dust again with flour and fold in half once more. Cut them into ½ in [13 mm] wide strips for fettuccine and ⅜ in [9.5 mm] wide strips for tagliatelle. Gently toss to separate the pasta. Store in the fridge for up to a few hours. To freeze, curl the pasta in four little nests, freeze on parchment paper, uncovered, until hard, then transfer to resealable bags and freeze for up to 3 months.

And that's what happens when you let a stand-up comedian, who really has no right to write a book, write a book.

<3 Matteo

Ricotta e Carciofo

Zucca

Renzo e Lucia
1959
la pasta più buona
che ci sia

Lasagna Funghi
e Piselli
ingredienti:
SEMOLA, UOVA, Olio di Oliva, Sale
Aglio, Cipolla, Funghi, Piselli MOZZARELLA,
PARMIGIANO REGGIANO, BESCIAMELLA

DA CONSUMARSI ENTRO IL
17/06/2024
Conservare in frigo da 0 a +4 C
LOTTO N.   06/14/24

2000021011502

pastarenzoelucia.it

CACIO e PEPE

Burrata

Cezn

Ricotta e Tartufo

Renzo e Lucia
1959
la pasta più buona
che ci sia

Lasagna al Ragù

ingredienti

SEMOLA, UOVA, Sale, Olio di Oliva, Cipolla,
SEDANO, MOZZARELLA, Carne Bovina,
Pomodori, PARMIGIANO REGGIANO

DA CONSUMARSI ENTRO IL
17/05/2024

Conservare in frigo da 0 a +4 C
LOTTO N. 08/14/24

2000169037006

pastarenzaelucia.it

Acknowledgments

This book could not have happened without the support of some special people.

This is for my mom, Cherie. Thank you, Mom, for nurturing my curiosity and encouraging me to create, draw, laugh, paint, sing, and cook. This book is dedicated to your endless sacrifices as a mother to me, Kate, and Vince.

Thank you, Dad, for letting me stay home with Mom to bake instead of dragging me out hunting and for embracing our big Italian-Mexican family that has filled our home with love (and a bit of chaos) for so many years.

Aunt Cindy, thank you for the gift of humor and for giving me a safe space to laugh and forget my worries. Uncle Mike, thank you for being like a second father, for enduring our jokes, and for always appreciating Aunt Cindy's cooking, even if pasta wasn't your favorite.

Thank you to my sister, Kate, whose strength and passion in life and in the kitchen inspire me every day. I love you, and I bet we'd make a great cooking show duo.

And to my cousin Brian, my kindred spirit, thank you for teaching me how to laugh—really, truly laugh. Your talent and intelligence continue to inspire me.

Thank you to my chosen family: Bob, Patti, Monet, Mitch, Jacob, Alfredo, Kennedy, and I guess Nick.

To my Rome crew, Francesco, Eleonora, Elena, Pietro, Tezeta, and Daniele: Mi dispiace di avervi fatto mangiare così tanta carbonara.

Thank you to Katie Parla for teaching me about Roman food and also being a badass.

And to Rodrigo, I can't believe you still have to listen to me talk about pasta. At least now you know chicken doesn't belong on pasta.

To my literary agent, Andrianna deLone, thank you for your faith in this project and for putting up with me and my schedule.

Tiffany Schloesser, Beth Stein, and Paige O'Donnell: the trio that keeps me alive. I love all of you. Thank you.

To Chris Caso for producing, filming, and editing every YouTube video and Insta clip. This book wouldn't be possible without our pasta project. And thank you to the friends who joined me on camera and cooked with me.

Thank you to JJ Goode. I will miss our meetings! The amount of time it took to describe to you how many different grandmothers I have . . . You're a killer. And to Laura Manzano, for your diligent recipe testing.

Antonis Achilleos and Vanessa Dina, thank you for coming all the way to Italy and capturing everything so perfectly, and thank you to Victoria Granof, Emanuela Rota, and Christopher White for all your incredible work.

Thank you to the entire team at Chronicle Books, especially my EXTREMELY PATIENT editor Dena Rayess, who was a vital part of making a book I love. Thank you to Michael Morris for bringing my vision to life. Thanks to the rest of the book team for making things happen behind the scenes: Jessica Ling, Wynne Au-Yeung, Tera Killip, Steve Kim, Erica Gelbard, and Elora Sullivan. Thanks to Emilia Thiuri, Margo Winton Parodi, and Lynda Crawford for your eyes on this book.

Side note . . . Why on earth did anyone let me write a book?

Index